SUPPORT INDEPENDENT BOOKSTORES

ELEPHANTJOURNAL.COM

For every #thingsIwouldliketodowithyou
bought on Amazon, we donate to
THE GREAT ESCAPE MUSTANG SANCTUARY

THIS BOOK BELONGS TO:

Things

I would like to do with You.

Waylon H. Lewis

BOOKS

BOULDER, COLORADO

A collection of loneliness & love.

To my mother

To Chögyam Trungpa

And to all those who find joy through service

I dedicate this story.

Second Edition. Any imperfections will make this book super-valuable.
ISBN: 978-0-9864273-0-5
eBook ISBN: 978-0-9864273-1-2

Printed and bound in the United States on chlorine-free 30% recycled 100% sustainably-harvested paper with vegetable-based inks and a plastic-free cloth cover. Distributed without Amazon. Every book karmically-offset by a donation to help a cute orphaned baby elephant via Sheldrick Trust.

For questions, bulk orders, or to book a reading with the author:
books@elephantjournal.com

Want to share your favorite chapter? Individual chapters appear in original form at: elephantjournal.com

To order a book, tee shirt, mug, sticker: elephantjournal.com/books
For daily inspiration: facebook.com/thingsiwouldliketodowithyou

Author's Note.

We no longer long for "happily ever after." We no longer believe in "you complete me" or *Mad Men* gender roles.

But we all, still, love to love love.

This book is an exploration of a love for a *new* generation— a love replete with intimacy and trust, a love with room for change and independence, a love without ownership.

I began this book rather casually, after a Midsummer Night's date. The first chapter met with more enthusiasm than anything I had ever written. It was then serialized on *Elephant Journal,* where it garnered millions of readers and an online community of 108,000. I felt like a donkey, who had accidentally won the love of a fairy queen—this new love is something we were all clearly puzzling over.

Things I would like to do with You is a universal, personal and timeless exploration of love—a love that includes loneliness, humor, and friendship.

May it be of benefit!

~ Waylon H. Lewis
Boulder, Colorado
Autumn 2015

Let's read.

Contents.

~

Preramble.

As we look to the sort of future love that we would like to hold—one that includes ample room for our loneliness and our love's independence and yet is full of our friendship—we look over our past relationships and remember their lessons in love. And a long line of the dear hearts who have loved us, however briefly, files slowly past and waves good-bye to us, one by one.

This story is not true, but it is not fiction. This story is my heart's life.

A cabin that is not a cabin begins this story that is not a story—though I do not yet know where I will find the cabin that will finish this story.

I have written this story out so that it will forget me; I leave our precious past in the stream beneath the trees.

I have taken my pen to white paper and scrawled black ink into the words of our red laughter: I take the winds of Nature's breath and invite them to carry my voice. And so I have written this story, and set it all out without saying anything extra.

~

I do not write these words to sound sickly sweet or saccharine: I write truth and whatever comes out comes out and I am this. And so I offer up this thin book for the fire: visible tracings of ephemeral experience.

And I must remind you that none of this is serious, it is only daydream, occasionally hot to the touch. If you are not here, you will only hear a bird's too-loud cheery morning song.

But one of you may strike a match to light up these dreams and these words may become real. Here are the scraps of paper: each chapter tells of past relationships until now, so that you will know all of me and so that I may let go of all and so that we may leap into our unknown futures.

This story is not linear: it is a hymn. This song is repetitive. It is a mantra that bears repeating, and I echo these seed syllables, humming yet more deeply.

As Fitzgerald said,

> *"Mostly, we authors must repeat ourselves—that's the truth. We have two or three great and moving experiences in our lives—experiences so great and moving that it doesn't seem at the time anyone else has been so caught up and so pounded and dazzled and astonished and beaten and broken and rescued and illuminated and rewarded and humbled in just that way ever before.*

Then we learn our trade, well or less well, and we tell our two or three stories—each time in a new disguise—maybe ten times, maybe a hundred, as long as people will listen."

So I sing these *Things*: a story of a heart full of sad trouble and revelry, and the opening of it—and it is that simple.

As a wise man once said, a warrior's duty is to attend to the heart and the opening of it—not as a task to be completed, but as a duty to be repeated daily in the orange glow of the new sun.

I would like to tell you my story, but it is not my story: it is ours. I would like to bring our book and read it to you. It was mine and it was hers, both, but since it is ended, it no longer belongs to either of us. It will not all be romance, it will be better: it will be ours.

None of this happened. But if it did happen, it would be with you and it would go like this.

chapter one.

Things I would like to do with You in the Woods.

"The simplest things are often the truest."
~ Richard Bach

I would like to go a way's away, to a Cabin, and I would like to look you in the eyes, and you look me in the eyes, as lovers do, a soft invisible smile—quiet, warm, calm. I would like to not come back for ten days (ten days is not long enough, but it is longer than I have taken for myself in eleven years). It would be a first visit, a return to the woods of my youth. I can cut wood quite well, and show you how. I can pick too much mint, because I am distracted by you. The mint is strong, almost bitter, in the wild.

I would like to walk with you in the moonlight. The grass is wet. I can see you clearly in the dark, only you are black and white, but I cannot see how the gate opens, so I have to feel for it, and the ground is uneven so…walking, talking, listening to and with you…I walk left then right, as if tipsy. The ground is not flat out here, and I love you. I mean, I love that about nature: it is uneven.

I would like to love you, but I do not know you, and I value space more than even love, for in space we can play. I would make a fort in our cabin out of sheets and we can go inside and just lie there. I am looking at you, into you, and you are looking at me, into me. And we could read a paperback. I have a good reading voice. And we could have a fire, though it is not cold, but it would light up the fort, flickering, warmly, with shadows of our future. I would like to love you and you love me, for love can only be shared, but my luck does not run that way, these days, or for awhile, and I have a feeling that I will not love and be loved again until all my luck is run out.

"A good traveler has no fixed plans, and is not intent on arriving." ~ Lao Tzu

I would like to talk with you about things I care about that others do not care about because they do not care about me, and hear you care, not because you care about me, but because you care about the things I care about.

I would like to listen. I could do it half the night, hour turning over hour, until I fall *asleepinyourwords*. I need to make up time:

I need to listen and breathe and take you in and just

stop.

I need to relax, and breathe—and what I need most (of course) is to cry. But you will not see my tears, for I cannot quite cry yet. The mosquitoes, the water roaring beneath us, your unwritten life set like calligraphy on a new page—arching, bright, sharp, wandering, struggling, fast, laughing. Letting go is half the beauty in elegance.

You are kind.

I would like to bring a cheap paperback with pen illustrations, say, and read it in the crook of a tree, and I would gingerly walk there barefoot, and you would be overdressed in a one dollar secondhand dress, as if going to a play. You would skip stones in the creek, then I would try and outdo you. You would set out a picnic, and a cold thermos of mint water, and I would eat your leftovers, and the trees far above would waver greenly in my eyes as I looked up at you looking up at them.

There is a yellow butterfly! On the book, waving its wings without flying, softly. I wonder what it is thinking about, today?

On the second-to-last night, I would like to make another fire, even though we do not need it for warmth: because it is Summer, and we have old wool blankets. But the flickering

flames, the shifting warm light, are the best light for talking, endlessly, as if we were at camp, and sex is not the only thing we humans can think about. And perhaps I could hold your hand. There is nothing better than holding a hand...feeling your fingers, your nails, your calluses, your palm. And your hand, held yet holding mine, feeling the stress and bruises of life, your strong fingers cautioning: *rest now, you are cared for.*

When I awaken I would like to meditate, with or without you, it is up to you. And I would like to do the samurai's calisthenics (I can show you how), and brush my teeth in the cold stream. And it is the woods, so I would not need to shave. But I might anyways, because sometimes it is doubly nice shaving in the woods; one's face pressed up near to an old little mirror over a wash basin set on a rickety Winter-worn wood shelf.

And I would like to make dark, dark coffee in a French press, but you are better at it.

I would like to care for you.

I would like to see you again, though I know you are, already, in love with another and so your love is not available to me. And the funny thing is, I do not mind. Perhaps when one has come over a long mountainpass, and is hungry, happy, beaten, and sad, and finally humbled, and lonely, perhaps then, sunshine is enough.

And perhaps, next time we could go for more than ten days, and never return.

"If your mind isn't clouded by unnecessary things, then this is the best season of your life." ~ Wu-Men

chapter two.

Things I would like to do with You this Evening.

"O, then, dear saint, let lips do what hands do;
They pray, grant thou…" ~ William Shakespeare,
Romeo to Juliet, upon first meeting.

I would like to ask you out.

I would ask you out to a play, or an outdoor concert, or a picnic—
something old-fashioned and slow and private, but outside.

Let's go to a play. You told me you have picked out your dress,
it is old. I have no idea what I will wear, and do not care.

I do care about your face, and your walk, and your voice, and
whether you read, and what. And that is the point of going out.
Getting to know. I want to know, among nine other things,
whether you have the guts to do your own thing.

I would like to ask you out. "Yes." But not romantically—

you are still not available, and I am not sure. I was wounded, and while I have soaked and healed and cried and talked and dated…I am a hardened young man, now, and no longer all so very young. I am not scarred: I am not scared of failure. But I am beaten, beaten, beaten like a sword in the fire. And as the smoke of karma has dispersed, I find that for the first time in my love life, sex is not a goal. Like a confettied champagne-soaked tickertape parade at the end of a great victory, I know it will come with, if the rest happens.

And I want to ride my invisible bicycle up to you,
sitting on a bench.

The rest begins now, though it may end in the next moment. Or this moment. That is how first and second dates are.

First dates are thin, eager, weak, sweet, young…full of real but ephemeral love. The tired heart warms again and, childlike, a naive hope of love buds up.

Second dates are a time to talk, a time to get to know—a time to see if the avocado soaked in clean water in a jam jar set on only two toothpicks in the warm sun will sprout. You have to wait two weeks, sometimes.

I am too old for naive optimism. I am too young to take myself too seriously.

I would like to take dance lessons with you, my hand on the small of your back.

I am good at laughing while learning and moving through crowds: a skill that comes in handy at festivals and parties and in leadership and in playing, as I did when I was a Beatle-headed boy with a stick, drawing lines in the rained mud so the streams of water would join or route this way or that. I used to spend hours saving the silly worms from blindly drowning in tiny puddles.

I would like to see how you dress: you like stripes, you like belts. You like silk, you like wool, you like cotton, cashmere, angora. And I would like to remember the color of your eyes before the dusk comes, and I would like to know whether to say your first name this way or that, and how to say your last name.

I would like to get to know you, more.

And if, in the dance of conversation and movement, we find ourselves swimming, cool jade saltwater, Fog City-like moisture beneath the wide moon, then we may wish to embrace. But we will not.

You like white, you like turquoise, you like buck-tanned boots.

Watching the play, I would like to be distracted by my desire to touch you. I would like to have to focus again and again on the actor's rapid, dense language. This is no comedy, no romance. My desire for you now is curious, it is careful, it is the kind of romantic desire that leads great writers to write timeless poetry and poor writers to write sweet drivel. For there is no greater joy known to humankind than in first holding hands—except,

~

perhaps, staving off the desire to do so.

And that may seem saccharine, but think: touching for the first time is the moment of—the passing from—"you are a human and I am a human and there are thousands of millions of others like you and me" to "you are a human and I am human and we are Us." This is an intimate moment that, like smoke from clean Japanese incense, is easily dispersed by a wave of the hand. Fate or a brief moment of argument or a chilling of insecurity or a lapse of presence and the spark of our enjoyment of one another may cool. It has happened before. And no one wants cold; everybody wants warmth. But I cannot hold your hand, not yet.

I want to know how many brothers or sisters you have, and are your old parents loving to you and one another, and how well do you love your friends, and how do you discuss ex-boyfriends who you still care for, or do not care for, or like, or do not like. And do you need drugs, legal or illegal, and why. And what music do you listen to, and a thousand other things like: your neck. Do you have integrity and an old soul, a mother's wisdom, and yet do you smile readily, like the jump of a deer, startled!

And I want to read your thank you card. And I want to read your thoughts and fall in love too much for just a moment. Then I pull back in. I will pass along your Mason jar of pickled beets to my friends who joined us (so rare and thoughtful of you), and I want to eat the other red gift, the one that is for me.

I want to see you from the right, and from the left. You prefer your left side. I prefer both (good god). I want to keep my mind and desire at bay: beauty demands focus, early on. Later, one can relax into it…

…as I do when it is snowing and I have had a long day and I sink into my hot tub with an *aaaaaaah*, and I have brought fresh coffee out with me if it is sunny or cold, local gin if it is dark, and I drink the first too quickly or I sip the second too slowly and yet I savor either. My cowboy hat keeps the snowflakes off of my wrinkled *New Yorker,* in which two of the articles are good enough to frame and put up on a wall where I might reread them, forever, and others might enjoy them when they stop by for some reason and wait in my entrance because they do not want to take their shoes off.

I would like to want you, but I do not know you, and I finally no longer want what I do not know.

It is true: I do not want you. I have not even thought of opening and kissing you and bending, holding and rocking you. I have thought (The Buddha's Heart Sutra)…I have always thought (and I am well aware that my thoughts are form, and empty, and luminous if seen as such) of your hair, your bow and arrow, your eyes, your hammer or saw, your pen or laptop, and your style, and your wide white smile, and your hand-writing. Your words make me want to savor you.

I have always been a champion for elegance.

I would like to slowly walk back to my house with you. I will kiss you good night, chastely, on the cheek, holding your left shoulder with my right hand. Later, not now, I would like to know (and if not, I would like to be true friends, and that would be a gift, too).

"Some may think only to marry, others will tease and tarry, mine is the very best parry—Cupid he rules us all." ~ a love song written for Romeo & Juliet.

I would like to daydream. And I would like to fly to you and with you. I would like to learn to surf and wear very little for a long time with you. I would like to jump off a modest cliff over a lake in the old green country with you, and dogpaddle and dry off. I would like to go to book readings with you, and wear white with you. And I would like to admire your stripes and literary sadness…and even grow old with you, and live in a proud yellow house and a humble cabin and I would like to raise ten children, or twelve, or three. With you.

I am an excellent uncle to many, and will make an excellent father, and a strong but silly, and almost-always patient husband. I will make a generous success of myself. And I will make a tireless, charming, stubborn public servant when my sideburns turn white and my eyes crinkle in the sun (like the old lonely friendly widower this morning on the mountain lookout who remembers when they put in the first stoplight).

I can promise a busy life, with peaceful moments. And a warm one, and a hard one, full of true lessons.

I would not like to: argue, but to debate. I want not to push you, but to be encouraged by you; I want not to be bored of you, but to laugh at myself. I want to walk behind you, closely following your golden shoulders and pregnant mind.

"Ooh, stay open…"

I would not like to: think about my walking, but to be present. I want to nearly forget to plan to go on future dates together, so lost are we together, but then to go to new old plays and have future unexpected times of discord and degradation of integrity only serve to highlight our woolen, romantic friendship within a Summer fort.

"I wanna make this play…" ~ Rhye

I would like to remember…how my voice grows soft around you. My soft voice surprises me, but not you, for you do not know my normal voice. I would like you to remember…your kindness surprises me: I am used to new friends and lovers feeling small around my whirlwind, soon beginning to tear at me for a superiority that I do not claim.

I would like not to want…no more, but to have…and to let go. The beets are delicious, this time of year.

I would like to see you.

"What is a youth? Impetuous fire.

What is a maid? Ice and desire.

The world wags on.

A rose will bloom

It then will fade

So does a youth.

So does the fairest maid.

Comes a time when one sweet smile

Has its season for a while…

Then love's in love with me."

~ that love song written for Romeo & Juliet, again.

Things I would like to Remember about our First Kiss.

"Often a man wishes to be alone and a girl wishes to be alone too and if they love each other they are jealous of that in each other, but I can truly say we never felt that. We could feel alone when we were together, alone against the others. It has only happened to me like that once. I have been alone while I was with many girls and that is the way that you can be most lonely. But we were never lonely and never afraid when we were together."
~ Ernest Hemingway, A Farewell to Arms.

I would like to be able to look back, some day far away, and remember these things. So I write them down, here, for me, for you.

I would like to remember my first sight of you in a lifetime.

Perhaps I will be visiting my childhood home out East, just

having flown in to the Old Harbor City where I went to college and having rented a car and now I am in this little state, surrounded by green hills, and memories. And you will drive over from a neighboring town where you are visiting for a few months, while building a tiny house for yourself.

This was my childhood home when I was young and sweet. I lived here, in this Buddhist retreat center, while attending an old-fashioned high school fifteen miles away.

Having known each other since I was small, and you were smaller, our parents know each other, and we speak the same familial language, the same dialect.

Hundreds of people still live here, and thousands of people still visit each year. People come here to study Buddhadharma, and wind up falling in love, and doing dishes, and living in tents or cramped little rooms. It is a big sprawling house with other big sprawling houses and meditation halls and a children's play area and a big kitchen and a big silver walk-in refrigerator with big blocks of cheese in it and a big barn-red barn and a gift shop. And all of it surrounded everywhere by vast waving green fields and a big garden and a long slow winding stream, below it all, and richly wooded hills, around it all.

I have not been back for twelve years.

It is sunny. And when you walk up and I first see you, I am playing basketball, just as I used to do, in a dusty big driveway, sweat stinging my eyes.

I am so happy, having finally returned. The sun is warm on my freckled shoulders. Shot after shot falls or fails: I am so happy to play here again, in this my old red and green valley home, that shots missed are as fun as shots made.

And I turn and there you are; all of you at once.

I would like to remember you walking up. Pale blue dress, tan corduroy gold cap with orange letters embroidered on it. You are new to me; all grown up. We knew each other here when we were younger, but it has been many years. And now you are tall. Light eyes, expressive lips. Golden.

A sudden physical manifestation of a hypothetical being. I am surprised by your reality, and relieved: you are beautiful. Beautiful is more than attractive—it means inside is as outside and we discuss this, later, in the night.

From out of the consequential mists of virtual communication, inspired by words, we have met and you are manifest.

I would like to remember that we hugged lightly and I kissed your wide cheek and I said this and you said that and I said, "You get lunch, I had a late breakfast. I'll keep playing."

Even in that first flush, space.

You go in and get food and you come out and sit on the old wide white farmhouse front porch where you can watch me. You sit with the tall thin gardener who we have both known

33.

since we were little.

And after awhile: sweating and gracefully shooting out my nervousness on the sand court, I stop.

I walk up above to the main house and shower in the same men's locker room I used to use when I was fourteen. I shower in three minutes without soap or towel, grinning at the memories in this sprawling old house.

Twenty jumping jacks in my shorts outside in the new sun and I am dry. I walk down and get a little lunch and a lot of home-made Tibetan Hot Sauce and join you, sitting on the old porch where so many of us have spent so many hours, for so many years.

A tall young man is talking to you, and the tall thin gardener and you and I, we all talk, and I eat and make jokes, and compliment the young man, and relax with you.

The young man wants to join us for our swim, later, and I look down at my food as I eat and wait—waiting to see if you are weak in your politeness.

You are not. But you are not rude, either, you simply demur. I am relieved at your strength and surprised by your skillful kindness. I gently smile at the young man and say that you and I would like to see each other one on one— "it's been years."

I would like to remember walking away with you to your little black car. You christened it Sodapop. I would like to remember our ready repartee, your quick laugh, my constant humor, your sweet voice, your thoughtful enunciation.

We meet well.

We ping pong back and forth, talking and sharing, learning and listening and interrupting…getting to know.

We drive along an old road through farms and fields…and we are not in a rush, and neither are the ten other small cars in front of us, driving fifteen miles an hour behind a tractor-trailer. It is rare, this not being in a rush: for we are both already where we want to be.

I would like to remember the feeling of old sights watering my parched memory—my eyes have not seen these turns, views, homes, barns for twelve years. But this being the country, it is all as if unchanged.

We laugh a lot. We park. I look at a few whiteblond-haired children preparing to swim, and feel the future looming against the present. I take refuge in the present: future is not real.

You change in the woods because the old bathhouse with the old changing rooms is locked, while I stare ahead at the timeless view of a wide lake with wooded hills framing a sandy beach on which children play and parents sit beneath tall green mountain trees.

This is a dream. None of this could really happen, again.

~

"You know you're in love when you can't fall asleep because reality is finally better than your dreams."
~ Dr. Seuss

I would like to remember this Lake, with you. How we find our halfsunny, halfshady spot beneath two trees, and you sit up in your bikini and I lean back in my trunks and we talk, laugh, laugh, talk, talk more and listen, and talk more and listen, and laugh more and listen…getting to know. So many questions.

"So how do you like me, so far?" I ask, out of the blue. I am serious, but relaxed now, and confident. You laugh at me. I appreciate your eyes, and your lips, and your voice, and your mind.

This morning I gathered nearly ripe purple-red plums. Now I take them out of my upside-down trucker hat (flip the bill into the back and it becomes a redneck purse) and eat five of them and toss the seeds into the bushes, vaguely wishing them to find soil and bury themselves and find water and birth new plum trees. And you eat one.

And again and again I bring myself back from my enthusiasm for this present moment with you: back to this present moment. It is hard: the joy of my longing is tart but sweet, I can taste it, but it flowers from the present moment and is rooted there, or rather here, so here I return.

And we go into the water. "I hope nobody notices I'm just wearing my underwear." I had not noticed, because I was trying not to look. "No one will." Your bra and your underwear are dark. But just to be safe, "I'll distract everyone." And so I run in, as I am wont to do anyways, knees high so I can run as far into the water as possible, and I splash and run and joy! And at last I jump and dive and slide into the still shallow water, and with practiced big broad strokes I swim out underwater just about as far as I can, which is far.

Finally, I surface…thousands of feet from the beach. But I can still stand: I am actually only one hundred feet out. And we swim and dogpaddle and stand and talk about love and loss and parents and seaweed and real estate and work and broken relationships, forever…getting to know. The sun warms us and the clouds shiver us and the water cuddles with us. And a fish tickles your legs, three times. The first time you yelp!

At one point you take out a sharp, perceptive knife and smoothly core my heart, "You get ahead of yourself. You think five steps ahead. I'm the opposite. I take forever to decide, I'm careful." And it is true, though I do not understand how you can already tell.

Finally we head back ashore. I swim underwater again: I love plowing through water, my shoulders remembering their forgotten strength. And we sit and talk for another forever: laughing, comfortable, sad. And we talk until finally you seem to want to move, and I ask.

And you say you would like to have ice cream, but I am vegan and I would not want any, and I say "ah I'm fine with other people having fun."

chapter three.

~

And you say you would still like that date with me that we had talked about over the past months, writing to one another. And I am pleasantly surprised that one such as you would like one such as me. I am not insecure, but I know myself, and in knowing ourselves we become fundamentally modest. And you are exquisite, and wise.

And I did not take you for a fool. But I am happy to be foolish with you.

Love is foolish, of course: as was last night's wide orange white fullish moon, illuminating a thundering waterfall in a small country town into glowing gray.

I would also like to remember our drive back through West Town, passing thirty young runners, and our stop at a general store (it carries saké, being close to our big old Buddhist home) so you could go to the bathroom. There is only one organic wine, and that is enough. And you offer to buy it, or pay your half. You drive me to my guest house, and you see the tall gardener who is hosting me, and while you two talk (you garden, too) I run upstairs and change into jeans: I know my old high school town and the locals do not need to see me in short shorts.

And: I would like to remember our drive up into the town of my high school days, where I get us to stop and browse at a store on Railroad Street that I like: the one with bright Pendleton blankets and French wine and local mead and sleigh bells that sound like water, and old-fashioned nighties, and thick cowboy shirts, and moose antlers, and red Persian rugs and Norman Rockwellish old prints. I could buy things there, and I do not often buy things.

But soon you shoo me out, because I am doing an interview with someone important in an hour. And so I belatedly realize that you expected our picnic date to be *before* my interview. There is not enough time for that, anymore; I had assumed we would date after. We drive to a natural grocery set in a former Church, and we do our picnic shopping.

I would like to remember how we decided to buy what for our picnic: dates 'cause we are on our date, and pistachios salted or garlic? Salted. And crackers but no let's get blue organic chips 8 oz not 6 oz, and hot salsa, it won't really be hot, the mainstream only buys "hot." And then Lily chocolate, yes chocolate is vegan if it's not milk, and olive tapenade *mmmm*, and pesto (love pesto), and kale salad, and stuffed grape leaves in a tin. And I joke with the cashier and we drive off, still talking,

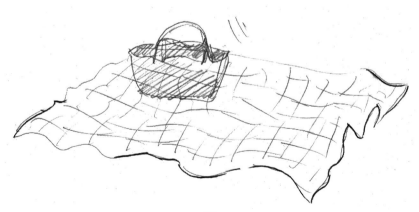

~

listening, our minds braiding our lives…getting to know.

We braided strands of our past into this present: we talked and listened and laughed about our hearts, our families, our disorganized religion, our friends and their new children, our limited memories of one another, my home and my dog, your sisters, the tiny house you are building, and your art and immediate future. We are just about friends, now.

And oh, yes—I would like to remember our first date. Sitting on green grass by the slow moving river then fast sparkling waterfall, the last sun of the day gold, slightly orange, I sit on my Filson coat, and you sit on your whiteblue towel and we spread out the dishes, and feast. We only have twenty minutes, yet we take those minutes slowly and live them fully. It is the best date I can ever remember perhaps ever, and I have had many good ones full of connection, humor, hope. But this: it is easy, romantic, just so. And somehow unrushed.

And we decide to save dessert (the dates, pistachios, chocolate, wine) for a second date, also tonight, after you set up your tent and after I finish my important interview.

And somehow I have not fucked it all up, yet, I think, as I walk away from you and your little car, and off to the work that is my love and life.

> *"I was about half in love with her by the time we sat down. That's the thing about girls. Every time they*

**do something pretty…you fall half in love with them,
and then you never know where the hell you are."
~ Catcher in the Rye.**

I would like to remember this second date in our date-work-date sandwich, as you called it.

We plan to meet on the porch again. I am late and there you are: "Sorry, the interview went long," but you have just arrived. And we walk up the hill to your tent, it is dark now, and we stumble on a root or rock but mostly we both know our way, having grown up playing in these hills.

Your tent, set on a wooden platform, has a screened-in porch safe from the flies and mosquitoes. I would like to remember our conversation. For in it I first found your strength, your earth, your way of articulating criticism: no rush. We do not

listen, wind.

have glasses, so we drink out of the bottle and I eat many dates, and we eat good chocolate, and I show you how (don't chew, just place on tongue, enjoy it as it melts) and you do not care. And our words or minds braid until even our hearts touch: everything is a joke, or sad. I ask about your comment that I am ahead of myself, I did not understand it though it sounds right.

I can feel myself falling in love with you; I dig in my heels to slow the fall.

For this love for you is not love, or for you: it is only enthusiasm. Instead, I will give you space. This is how: I return to this moment, where all tensions are solved by not needing resolution, and I listen to you, and make jokes, and share. And yet still I fall in love, knowing it is not real. We will find out how deep the roots wend, if this is more than just mutual projection.

But not tonight.

We talk about private things. You are brave in your openness. And I am open; this is one thing that is easy for me.

And I would like to remember that we watched the yellow moon rise behind the black trees. And the occasional flashlights bobbing up the low mountain trails.

I ask if I can hold your hand.

I would like to remember that you laugh at me for asking. And I would like to remember how I first touched one of your long hands. And how your fingers enthusiastically yet sweetly explored mine. And how my strong relaxed hand held yours. You have calluses. You laugh when I kiss one of your hands, so in a bad French accent I threaten to curtsy, next—"that's my deal-closer."

As we talk, our hands wander but only slightly, and finally I do not ask: we kiss.

It is our first kiss, so we take our time.

I would like to remember our first kiss.

"Sometimes when I look deep in your eyes I swear I can see your soul." ~ James

We kiss more, more. I kiss your top lip, a slight bite, your neck. And more. My failure to shave begins to hurt your face and lips. My hand in your nightdark hair and on your chin and your sharp hips and smooth shoulder. And we talk as we do this. And I interrupt you with a kiss: it is fun to interrupt when the interruption is welcome. And I lay you down and I lay beside you and over you and we talk, kiss, more, more, and I touch your sternum, which is close to your heart.

And you touch and kiss me, but I do not pay attention to me, I pay attention to you.

Time happens.

~

You decide that I will leave: it is too "dangerous" to stay.

I look forward to the moonlit long walk, though I fear the giddy joy after a first date: joy always precedes heartbreak.

Just before I leave your tent you say something like:

"I may seem impenetrable—but I have to ask you to be careful with my heart."

"Well, two things. One, yes, I will—and I appreciate that you asked. But I do not see you as impenetrable, and: please be kind to mine, too." But I say it in many words. "And, that's just the first part," I say, and you laugh. I have been jokey all night, almost too. "And the second part," I say, "is it actually could be good."

We walk out into the night and it is rich, dripping with joy.

And I thank you for this delicious privilege, which is to spend an evening with you in the woods.

And we walk down and hold and kiss. Your eyes are closed in the moonlight, eager lips.

I would like to remember my long, long, long walk home along familiar country roads over, along, down, up, left, down, across the river, along, beneath two bridges, and to. All beneath the bright white moon. Arriving at the gardener's farmhouse, I go upstairs to my attic room, meditate, and I work. Finally I fall asleep, fast and deep.

"The sun loved the moon so much, he died every night to let her breathe."

None of this may mean a thing, and you are nervous, and you want space. It may mean something, and I am not nervous, and I will give you all the space you need. For love if true is caring about another's heart, not merely one's own.

But: I would, too, like to remember the next day, and our talk in the water in the stream, you have had a long night of worry, you tell me—while I feel only joy and sun and slept well.

Your nervousness. You have closed, a cautious flower to the cool night. And my joy turns to sadness as sunshine makes way for rolling fog. Seeing my sadness, you tell a generously sweet, funny story. I ask: "Did you just tell me that story to cheer me up?" It is rare for a beautiful girl to care about the heart she stabs, even as she pierces it.

Our planned dinner date is late, and short, and we do not return to the tent, or laugh, or kiss or touch, much. I say you are not responsible for my sadness, I'm a big boy, and I will give you space. "But space can be *in* love, not just without it." But you do not hear my words. They are just words. You say, "I can't let you in."

I would like to remember the final good-bye: "Do what you want," you tell me, in that voice hearts use when they have closed.

"Ooh, stay open."

45.

~

And you say you may visit. And I say I will not ask for it. And we part.

And I sing all the way home, so that I do not drown in self-pity:

> *"Ohhh the winnnnter it is past, and the summmmer's come at laaast. A-and sma-all birds they sing on every tree-ee-ee…and the hearts of these are glaaad, bu-ut mine it is very saaad, for my truuuue love is pa-arted from me-ee-ee.*
>
> *Oh you who are in love, and cannot it remove, I pity the pains you enduuure…for experience lets me know that your heart, it is full of woe, a pain that no mortal can cure…"* ~ *Rabbie Burns, one of ChögyamTrungpa's favorite songs. (I have loved and sung it my whole life.)*

Things I would like to do with You in Time.

"We lead our lives like water flowing down a hill, going more or less in one direction until we splash into something that forces us to find a new course."
~ Arthur Golden

You are out there and I am out here and this is not the time.

But the time may come to pass: that is how time works. The only question that matters now, then, is whether our hearts have connected, and can learn to breathe together.

If you had a spare hour, I would not want to see you. I would want you to take a break from your path and do something lovely for yourself. A massage, or a swim, or fun with friends… whatever you have not done for yourself that you are thirsty for. *Maitri.* Space is love and I give that which cannot be given to but can only be taken from you. And you need it: as you have said, it provides ground for good things to come.

If you had a day, I would fly anywhere in the country to see you, if only for an hour, and we could drink warm hot brown coffee and go for a walk, and I would like to cry at the thought of seeing you and holding your hand, sitting on a bench, looking into the street together, seeing your profile from the other side. Sighs are healthy, for they mix watery emotion with space and humor.

If you had a week, I would like to meet you somewhere— on your road, or in my hometown. We could dinner and go to a show and to a bar and play pool and laugh at each other and drink local beer and stay separately or together. I would rent something where we could climb to the roof. We could bicycle and go to a used bookstore and we could cuddle, and read out loud, if that is not too much. If that is too much, we could just walk in the park. If that is still too much, we could just go to a party, and be loud and fun and barely make eye contact, but warm one another in each other's fires. If that is too much, we could just be naked, and sweat, and learn one another's bodies and movements, like two new surfers learning to respect the water.

If that is too much, we can forget one

another, mostly, as we have our other lovers.

If you had two weeks, we could go on a little break, together, to a romantic retreat—Big Sky, or Ocean Cliffs, or Pink Desert—with nothing but space, big skies, warm waters, nothing to do but be.

If you had three weeks, however, we should go to Blue Islands. White walls, blue walls, white sky, white sea, blue sea, blue skies. Your eyes. Your hair. Your bikini, my shorts, four tanned and sandy bare feet. What are the colors there? Blue, bright blue, pale blue, bluegreen, grayblue, bright pink flowers and sun, light pink and white tablecloth, white, white, white... I want to spend some time on the sea and in the islands. A painted lacquered wooden boat, your red dress. Impossibly blue sky and water. See-through white curtains in a hot breeze.

But if you had four weeks, and you were ready, which you are not, we should just be simple, together, in my hometown, and live life, and not do anything but hike, and drink coffee, and work, and laugh with my dog, and eat good food with many good friends, or alone, and climbrun together up along the creek into the mountains. We could text and make appointments with one another: "What are you doing later?," and see each other when convenient. Like adults, like normal life, and see.

And that would be the best—to live everyday life with you. For I do not know you and though I seem dreamy and open, just beneath that layer I am waiting, my hope balanced with *prajna*. Three layers down, I am rational: that is where my hesitation and patience rest. But I am not afraid of exploring and finding out what lies over the edge of the flat earth, for it is not flat.

I am not afraid of anything but filling your space. You need and deserve that and I would not like to be a part of anything other than love in your life.

And as you and I both know, in our bones, in our blood, in our mindstream, in our calm moments…love is made up of space just as the earth is made up of water.

And my love includes laughter. The woodfire requires wood and oxygen, both. And I love to cut wood.

Things I would like to do with You Before I Lose You.

"For true love is inexhaustible; the more you give, the more you have. And if you go to draw at the true fountainhead, the more water you draw, the more abundant is its flow." ~ Antoine de Saint-Exupéry

I would like to grow old with you, before I lose you.

You may lose me, first, for I am not all so very young, anymore. But I will take care of myself so that I may build thin bonfires on the cold beach beneath the country's deep sky's bright stars. I will climb regularly, I will wear through expensive running shoes running the hills with Red dog ("half-hound, all trouble"), I will bicycle every day no matter the weather, I will yoga (reluctantly, for it stretches me where I am tight—leaning into resistance makes me lazy). I will eat real food and go to bed at a reasonable hour (putting my work away and taking

Red dog.

up a book). I will not take my stress too seriously: I am good at walking away, sighing and laughing. For I would like to live to see your life. You will grow old like a thick vine, still flowering.

I would like to see you wear that turquoise dress with white flowers when your hair has turned white.

I would not like you to cut your wiry hair, but to wear it long: proudly but messily the way beautiful old women who like to garden or make art do.

"Looking into the world
I see alone a chrysanthemum,
Lonely loneliness..."

I would like to make love to you, and again, my tired head on your breasts, and again, my strong arms and shoulders lifting your hips up and rocking them, again, both hands turning you and pulling you and finally crushing down into you, again, my sweat and weight upon you. And again: for sex may get boring, but making love does not get boring, but it does get more and more intimate.

I would like to give you small gifts for no reason: like an old Oscar Wilde or William Blake book or a spontaneous, forgettable haiku with one too many syllables tacked up above the dishes that reminds you to relax or finish your art for I am picking up the children.

I would like to look at these children and feel a mixture of pride and relief in their health and beauty, and kindness and lack of self-consciousness. Little knights.

I would like to notice you noticing other men and remember that I do not own you, or hold you, or have you: I am a train, running alongside your tracks.

And I will not smother you, but I will smother them—with the paper-thin friendliness of a tiger, burning bright.

I would like to notice you ignoring them, too, as I do two moments after a beauty catches my gaze. For we both remember

~

that we have a thing so rare: we are best friends and skilled lovers, both…we help one another to laugh at ourselves.

"I stand like the lonely juniper

Which grows among rocks,

Hardened and tough.

Loneliness is my habit—

I grew up in loneliness…

Yet sometimes also,

Lonely moon,

Sad and Happy

Come together…"

I would like to love you. I would like to love you after the honeymoon. I would like to fight with you and dislike you and judge you and fault you…and remember to breathe and leave. And I would like to quickly fault myself and regret it all and go for a long hard walk, stomping in the woods. And I would like to come back and apologize and mean it, mostly.

And I would like to learn from you even as I argue with you, and even if I know you are somewhat wrong, and even if I know I am somewhat wrong.

I would like to stare into your eyes and I would like to cry but I will not. I have spent so many years trying clothes on, that when we set our hearts next to one another and found no fitting necessary—but rather we found you slow and me fast and both of us set against one another in delight: friendship shot full with passion—oh, I knew then that we had something more than a love affair.

I would like to take you out of the red woods and talk with you in the wood-paneled café with a fire lit in the dark stove. This Winter, after a chocolate tasting at a golden old bookstore, I ask you, and you say *yes*. This is before I lose you.

I would like to go on a first date with you, a VIP party, and see you melt into me…until my bad whiskey makes me dull and your interest slows and I just want to go home and I lose you.

I would like to make love to you, and again, and again:

I would like to take you upstairs, lifting you up onto my standing lap and seeing you, later, lying on the bed, open. And too readily take you then, again. But you take me first, in, and you take me to a honeyed dreamworld and I am lost in you.

I would like you to think to "spice things up," standing, touching your toes.

I would like to make love into you in the moonlight, you trying to coo softly so as not to wake up the neighbors.

I would like for the loud neighbors on the other side to finally holler in hypocritical anger at three in the morning

~

when you have been screaming, we are indoors, now, even
so: and for us to laugh and close the window, it is so hot,
I need air, so much sweat. I would like for you to pause
as I, from behind, first move with you and you pause to tie
up your thick curling hair out of your face.

I would like to watch you walk down the hall, tall, in front
of me, naked but for your underwear.

I would like you to ask me to leave my work and
rendezvous in the middle of the day for afternoon sex,
"It is the best."

Camping with friends: I would like to stuff the soft edge of
my hand or our pillow or our sleeping bag in your mouth,
we are trying to be quiet again, and again failing, your
head pushed against the edge of the tent, we are both
laughing and busy groaning as you open your innermost
to me in yearning delight.

I would like to draw you in graphite, and paint you
in purple, sitting cross legged, wearing very little, on our
poor couch.

I would like to be surprised by your honesty and wisdom
and your willingness not to understand yourself, but to wait,
and then to leap as much as fifty feet off the cliff and into the
water. You communicate, and are not selfish or cowardly in
your decisions.

I would like to dance with you, but not in slow-motion.

I would like you to stop laughing at me and let me take my dancing seriously: relationships must view one another in the fresh light of a morning white with sunheat but cool with breeze, or we risk fixing one another in our expectations and we live down to those expectations. And life if stale makes a relationship unsustainable.

I would like to move into and against you in the middle of an enthusiastic crowd and later we will walk to the parking lot and I will lean against you, leaning against a car. It is not our car, I bicycled.

I would like us to not play games, but rather to simply be honest no matter what.

It is a simple rule: good or bad, happy or sad, talk it out to me and it will all be alright.

I would like us to play games like Scrabble, or Trivial Pursuit, at the tap room, sitting in the tall golden booths with dear friends, drinking hoppy beer. I will eat spinach salad with walnuts and balsamic and nachos with beans and black olives and lots of hot sauce and extra jalapeños.

Before I lose you, I would like to see you again.

I would like to hike with you (and Red dog) up to the wide pale grassed park beneath the tall walk-stopping mountains and then up and then down another mountain where I played Malvolio and Ferdinand when I was a boy, in the red rock amphitheater built by FDR's peaceful army. Or I would like to

chapter five.

~

bike with you all the way up to the little mountaintop cowboy town for folkfiddling music; or I would like to go to an outdoor movie with you, someone brought their own couch; or to a fancy upstairs dinner, the kind you imagine having when you are twelve and you think about being grown up; or to farmers' market on Wednesday afternoon or Saturday morning between the creek and the museum.

I would like to run into you on the street and flirt at you and have you talk over me and laugh, for you are strong like a filly, and you laugh into me as I talk back over you, and we talk over one another as the tide does when it retreats and folds up against itself, old waves relaxing back into new waves rushing.

Before I lose you I would like to go to a bad poetry reading where everyone talks loudly and humorlessly, spoken word-style, because that is what they think poetry sounds like. When, really, we will smile at one another, for we know what poetry sounds like: it sounds like *this*. Close your soft eyes and listen. It sounds like listening to whales, underwater, on an old vinyl record in my childhood living room, in my memory. It sounds like the nightly crickets we forget to hear. It sounds like the pause before a cherished old song comes on: say, Supremes, or Debussy or Chopin, or Gene Kelly, or some jig. It sounds like old travels and old streams and six of us going for a walk on a straight dirt road after dinner.

I would like to hold your hand. For it is always the first time, when I hold your hand. For I am so enthusiastic about you that I hope you do not notice, and I have to constantly remind myself that I will lose you.

For the future is all made up, none of this matters, these are just words.

I would like to stop wordplaying, and see you.

"Never, never trust…"

I would like to belatedly protect you without jealousy or anger, and I would like to debate with you about astrology or Tarot or Mercury Retrograde or the effing Supermoon and I would like to be right but lose the argument, but not give in. And I would like to cuddle with you, despite the late Summer heat sweating us into one another…still we hold and fall asleep, the heat makes for tired hound dogs, lanky, napping.

> *"But be friendly.*
>
> *By being friendly toward others*
>
> *You increase your non-trusting.*
>
> *The idea is to be independent,*
>
> *Not involved,*
>
> *Not glued, one might say, to others.*
>
> *Thus one becomes ever more*
>
> *Compassionate and friendly.*

Whatever happens, stand on your own feet

And memorize this incantation:

'Do not trust.'"

~ Chögyam Trungpa

I would like to insist on staying with you when you give birth, though I am not good with blood from those I cherish, and I will faint nearly and be a bother and be asked to leave and go watch fuzzy television in the waiting room but I will stay and faint and be a bother.

I would like to read your handwriting and I would like to notice the way your eyes curve, and your wide white smile, and your simple yet personal style, and I would like to ask you the same damn questions again and again so that you wonder aloud if I do not listen but, no, I assure you without reassuring you: I have always been forgetful and it does not mean that I do not care.

I would like to grow old with you, before I lose you.

chapter six.

Things I would like to Hear from You when You are Afraid.

"Any confusion you experience has within it the essence of wisdom automatically. So as soon as you detect confusion, it is the beginning of some kind of message.

At least you are able to see your confusion, which is very hard. Ordinarily people do not see their confusion at all, so by recognizing your confusion, you are already at quite an advanced level.

So you shouldn't feel bad about that; you should feel good about it.

You should not be terrified of your confusion, but you should look into it further. You should push into it instead of closing yourself off. In that way, you just keep

*opening and unfolding, like flowers in the summertime.
Even though they are exposed to the weather, to the
wind and rain, flowers still keep unfolding themselves,
until finally they bloom at their best.*

*You could be like the flowers: you could let the bees sit on
you and take your honey away, and that would be fine."*
~ Chögyam Trungpa

I would like to communicate with you about difficult things.

Love can survive fear only if acknowledged.

Things are not easy, always. A love affair is not imagination. It is
the vicissitudes of daily life. It is two lifestreams intermingling.
It is heavy silence with nothing to say. It is inadvertently making
big deals about small nothings.

~

I would like to hear you give voice in the hard times—then I can know this is a river of true love, and not merely a shallow standing pool.

Love is not fantasy, it is bricks and mortar. Relationship is earth.

Love is fantasy, too. It is heaven: dreams and hormones and the pleasure in biology and sudden laughter.

It is the rub between the two that creates sparks: earth striking against heaven.

It is communication that is water that cools those sparks, and gets us through the fear of loss, the difficult times, the simple arguments over dishes or the serious arguments over ethics.

> *"What is required of us is that we love the difficult and learn to deal with it. In the difficult are the friendly forces, the hands that work on us. Right in the difficult we must have our joys, our happiness, our dreams: there against the depth of this background, they stand out, there for the first time we see how beautiful they are."*
> *~ Rainer Maria Rilke*

We have connected.

I would like to love you if that is how it is. I would like to honor this connection with mutual openness.

~

Or, I would like to lose you if that is how it is. I would not like to dishonor our connection with a lack of communication about the confusing things.

Connection is a rare spark, a cause for joy. I would not like to lose said spark because of your inability to communicate about your fear.

I learned when young that if confused I should be open about it, and it will get better.

And yet sometimes I forget this lesson: I collapse into insecurity, and if unopened it can become depression. When I cannot be charming, when I cannot be who you or others think I am, I am embarrassed.

It is our task to talk when we would hide. We can talk confusion, we do not have to wait for clarity.

I would like to honor our fear by tending to it. When gripped by confusion do not shut down: rather, talk it out.

It is a clumsy, simple tactic that works every time: by giving voice to that which I do not understand, my confusion gains sanity instead of calcifying into fear—fear, of fear.

If you are afraid, come here and I will hold you. Or go away, go for a walk and hold yourself, sweetly.

I would like to never resent your fear—if communicated. Rather: I would like to admire you for acknowledging your hesitation. There are reasons for it that I cannot yet know. And

I would like to care if you will let me see.

I would like to care more about you than about my feelings for you.

> **"Whatever occurs in the confused mind**
>
> **is regarded as workable.**
>
> **It is a fearless proclamation;**
>
> **the Lion's Roar."**
>
> ~ *Chögyam Trungpa*

Oh, I would not like this to be wonderful only to see it collapse, only because of broken communication. If we are not right for one another or the timing is not right and we cannot make it right, that is that.

Love is the hardest sport. Love is only available to those willing to be continually brave in weakness.

Can you be brave?

Say we have one wonderful night: say we bicycle far off together, to a wedding dinner with many ladies and gentlemen outside on a green farm. And say we laugh and dine at a white table amongst many white tables set beneath the gathering stars of a night that fast turns the green farm dark blue. And say you are elegant, and I will undress your elegance. But first in candlelight

~

we talk with mentors and parents of friends and then dance, dance, silly, enthusiastic, confident. The mosquitoes come out, hungry, we kiss and hold and talk and laugh, lying in the grass beneath the cool bushes lining the dark periphery of the bright tent.

It is an honor to know you.

But then, say, the next day you cancel our plans for our first dinner date without telling me. Thoughtfulness is a basic courtesy we extend to friends. And then, say, we gather that night with friends and you are with a gentleman and you sit over there and it is all an affront served cold. I do not revel in heated jealousy and I will soon be cooly fine with this loss of our warmth of the night before. Perhaps you slept badly and you are just out of a long uneven relationship and you are not ready to unfold your wings. I do not know and cannot since you do not tell me.

"To conceal anything from those to whom I am attached, is not in my nature. I can never close my lips where I have opened my heart." ~ Charles Dickens

And so I would like to fold *my* wings closed against your heart. Such cowardliness is for children, though children have an excuse.

I would like to breathe out into the rain and lightning night as

I bicycle away from you. I have made friends with myself, so I do not often fear loneliness. I am fine with disrespect, for my capacity to cease to care is contextualized by my good friend's repeated advice over the years:

"If she does not communicate, forget her, you deserve better."

Say, I would like to forget you.

> **"Happiness is not a goal; it's a byproduct of a life well-lived." ~ Eleanor Roosevelt**

I would like to love fully.

I would like to love my life and help you to love yours. Love is not selfish love but rather caring for another, which means we help to nurture our fundamental kindness.

That day may be far off but I do not think it is for I want to name twelve noble children foolish things like Margaret (Daisy) and Huckleberry and Winslow and Whitman and Washington and Kerouac (Cary, for short) and Roosevelt (Rose) and Thoreau and Sargent and…

I would like to love someone who would like to communicate.

I would not like to, say, call or text or email or message you and not hear back…I would not like to play games. I would not like to ask you out, and never be asked out. I would not like to treat,

~

and never be treated.

I would like us to not play games, but rather I would like for us to be simply honest.

"Becoming 'awake' involves seeing our confusion more clearly." ~ Chögyam Trungpa

Love is not one-way: that is for boyish *Mad Men* and bored Housewives, and I admire neither.

If you are busy, take your time: space is yours and I will not take it from you, and space is mine and I will not give it up for you. But: if you play games with communication, like old climbing rope my affection for you will fray.

Loneliness is the salve for love lost, and this antidote comes conveniently after misuse. I would not like to date a girl.

"And the day came when the risk to remain tight in the bud was more painful than the risk it took to blossom." ~ Anaïs Nin

I would like to love and be loved by a deeply sane human, brave enough to surf fear and voice it messily.

I am ready for love; I have seen many shadows of it, shadows so weak they cannot block the sun of your hot heart.

And I would like you to know that (so far) I am so grateful, I am tired, wet from the salt spray, I have stood by the shore all day and all my adulthood, day after day and some nights. But now I am ready to kiss the heart of a woman brave enough to feel fear and give voice to it. In voicing our fears we introduce oxygen and in so doing give our fires life. And yet I shall fondly look back at those times of loneliness at the water, the rock of the deep ocean, the creak of the wood that buoys me, the feeling of my tired hands shaking against the oars as I pull again, again against strong waves.

I do not want my idea of you.

That is too easy, and it is not real.

I want you, faults and all.

And I want you to want me, faults and all, not any ideas you have about love.

chapter seven.

Things I would like to Whisper
to You.

"Dance by the Light of the Moon.

Don't matter if the road is long

Don't matter if it's steep

Don't matter if the moon is gone

And the darkness is complete

Don't matter if we lose our way

It's written that we'll meet

At least, that's what I heard you say

A thousand kisses deep…"

~ Leonard Cohen

If you read my words and if you are excited, remember that I
do not know you—not really. If you read my words and you are

upset, and if you said you did not want to read them anymore, I would like to remind you that these words are not about you.

Except for the sweet parts.

I am a lover of love and I am a lover of words, and the two together spin visions of airy castles, but also may pierce the heart of hope. And so I remind you that I am a fool, a poet, and what matters is reality, not lovely words. Words are full of promise, yet empty of matter.

And: you may not want to read this one, either.

I will not share this one with you, but if you find it in a book, know that my love is *vajra*: pregnant with space, replete with strength and discernment, golden and heavily beautiful and threatening, yet a tool of use, for you.

For if I love you without knowing you these are just words, the kind of frustrating love where two people say "I love you," to one another, and mean it.

But it could be the kind of love, just possibly, perhaps, that goes unsaid. And so I shall unsay it unto you: I may possibly love you, in the way an ancient underground spring courses its invisible way below us, unseen, unknowing.

So I do not love you, and you do not love me. But it goes without saying, for it remains unsaid: I do not love you, and you cannot yet love me.

But I hear the spring, below.

It is nearly now Fall:

"I wanna make this play

Oh, I know you're faded

Hmm, but stay, don't close your hands

Caught in this pool held in your eyes

Caught like a fool without a line

We're in a natural spring

With this gentle sting between us." ~ Rhye

I would like to see you.

I would like to see you without you being seduced or pressured. I would like for us to feel only space and desire, the parents of bravery and curiosity. I would like you to want to see me.

I am not interested in playing games: games are for winners and losers and I do not ever want to win against you, or for you to lose against me, and I do not want to lose against you or for you to win against me. For we are part of the whole, the main, as Donne said—and your gain is mine and my loss is yours.

Love is about finding one's match: we shall touch our minds and hearts together at once, and never condescend nor aim for any goal between us but the truth.

"No man is an Iland, intire of itselfe; every man

is a peece of the Continent, a part of the maine;

if a Clod bee washed away by the Sea, Europe

is the lesse, as well as if a Promontorie were,

as well as if a Manor of thy friends or of thine

owne were; any man's death diminishes me,

because I am involved in Mankinde;

And therefore never send to know for whom

the bell tolls; It tolls for thee."

~ John Donne, Meditation XVII, Devotions
upon Emergent Occasions.

I do miss seeing you. It has been a lifetime.

I have no interest in a relationship of words. I miss you and you do not seem to understand this and I cannot blame you: for you are busy with your projects and to-do lists and friends and loved ones and past and nervous possibility of new things. Meanwhile I stand atop my castle, for I have fought my way up here and I am older, yet unbowed. I do not fight down below, I am not interested in petty skirmishes, for I hold all the advantage, up here: let your sweet battle come to me.

I first noticed you when I saw your strong hands pull Diana's golden bow. Like that independent Goddess, you are contented and self-contained and I would lose you through impatience, but I shall win you through fire, and when I win I shall offer up any reward for I would not like to play to win or lose in love with you.

As I wrote you, I would like to cry with you. I can cry, now. For many years I never cried. For more than a decade, I cried perhaps twice. Now I cry a few times a year, but rarely for long. But with you I could finally cry blue tears.

I would like to make love into you, naked, breathing, candles— unembarrassed because we are here together. It is not physical, it is…I would like to know you where that spring courses, pure dark water flowing; I would like to take your hand and swim down with you as deep as any two have ever dived and, down below, I would like to make love into you, and I would like you to make love over me.

> *"What is it you want, Mary? What do you want?*
> *You want the Moon? Just say the word and I'll throw a*
> *lasso around it and pull her down. Hey, that's a pretty*
> *good idea. I'll give you the Moon, Mary. Then you*
> *could swallow it and the moon beams would shoot out*
> *of your fingers…and your toes and the ends of your*
> *hair…am I talking too much?"*
> *~ George Bailey, It's a Wonderful Life.*

Though I am worthy of you, your fire confuses me.

~

If I lose you through my idiocy and impatience, well, that is your fault. For you should know I am an idiot and impatient and that, beneath your sun, I cannot stand to be indoors in the cool stale shade. It is like putting a wild horse in a corral: it is not right.

If I can see you, oh please let me: I shall be open. I am not vulnerable, you are not vulnerable, it is worse than that—I am like a mango peeled open: sticky, ripe. I am here for you. But you are *vajra*, too.

Our openness is our solidity.

My castle is impenetrable but I do not lock the front door. I leave my table and put down my pen for I do not wish to write many more romantic words. And I look out my window.

"She'll be comin' 'round the mountain when she comes."

And I can feel you coming to me.

I wish to breathe silent words into your ears that convey something of my understanding that life is short and precious and I intend to benefit all of society, and that I require a match, a princess, a fellow troublemaker with whom to make love and mischief. And even if our affection is bluegray friendship or even if our pinkpurple love lasts only a minute, you must know that I will treasure that time. And if I do not see you, you ought to be arrested: for you must know that I cannot live long without your sun, once introduced. Please pour into me your spring water or please sun me with your orangegold eyes.

And if you are busy or if now is not the time that is fine—for you. For me—I shall wither into myself, hard as the old vine. I shall still bear fruit to serve thousands of noble warriors, but I shall not be excited.

I lock my door to love affair; I only want full heart.

Do not read this, do not read this, for it is too much and I want to be too little (as you wish).

Ah: my warning to you to not read this came at the beginning, so if you are still reading, we have already won.

We cannot play games when it comes to this love: and this is how we shall win.

> *"I hear their voices in the wine*
>
> *That sometimes did me seek*
>
> *The band is playing Auld Lang Syne*
>
> *But the heart will not retreat*
>
> *There's no forsaking what you love*
>
> *No existential leap*
>
> *As witnessed here in time and blood*
>
> *A thousand kisses deep."*
>
> *~ Leonard Cohen*

Things I would like to do with You when You Visit my Home.

"Knowing how to be solitary is central to the art of loving. When we can be alone, we can be with others without using them as a means of escape." ~ bell hooks

I would like to see you.

It has now been too long. I saw you last month, and four days ago, and a year ago exactly: then I was flooded and now I am parched.

I would like to see you in just a few days when you arrive at my door: and, like children arriving for their first day of school, we will giddily greet this unknown new present with sweet shaky smiles. You will have arrived from no place. No home now but the road: driving from your old ocean home, to our old forest home, to her home, to my home in this flooded mountain valley, and then on into your future.

Where is home?

Your visit will not be long enough, which is the perfect length. Unless it is too long: *even better*.

We can do whatever we like. Perhaps we can eat at my favorite table at a favorite restaurant—I like it because it is outside but shaded, so I can see the sunshine as I work away my life on my laptop. I like it because it is a big table, from which I can see life pass me by on the sidewalk; and I like it because the big table is hidden, so I can work without too many folks stop n'chatting at me. We can get dark kale chips all over our teeth. We can eat a big salad or garlic potatoes with dijon and drink well-sourced seven-minute black coffee or kegged white wine and a local lager because there is nothing hoppy.

～

Perhaps—

> (*my hometown was just flooded, many homes lost and
> streets torn open and lives ruined and lives reborn…so I
> and many have been volunteering to help, and in so doing
> turning isolation and loss into community and relief. And
> dealing with my own drowned house asked a good deal of
> me: joy, sadness and stress. And I nearly got sick. And I let
> go of four pickup truckloads of soggy stuff—though I only
> miss the memories, not the things. And then one morning,
> waking up, I helped my neighbor lift mudwet hay bales
> without taking time to stretch or coffee or meditate first,
> and my back muscles spasmed, turning me into a tin man*)

…perhaps if I am feeling better we can run up and around and
down the mountains in the morning with Red dog.

Or I would like you to drive me into the mountains, if we can
find mountain roads that are open and dry, and we can get lost at
fourteen thousand feet and see the lakes reflect the heavens, the

⁓

air so clear up there. Or perhaps I can take you climbing, we will bike along the bike path, or we can play pool and drink good beer in a dark bar or perhaps we can see good friends on the damp lawn on Saturday morning, at farmers' market. Or perhaps we can drive to Cow City and visit a hipster dinner spot I love, or we can walk a museum or go to a fundraiser or film or cook at home and dress up for no one and light a candle and watch an old movie.

I have a list of things I would like to do with you.

It has not been a month, or a week, or four days. It has been my whole lifetime since I have seen you. I have sailed out to sea every morning, waking when it is still dark. The stars light against the cold sky, unraveling what my wiry hands had coiled up the night before. It has been too long, so long that I did not know you until I met you and said good-bye again to you—a lifetime without your friendship. I would like to see you.

But I would like to have been alone for these many years.

Alone gives me strength, stability and clarity in my direction. I have tried on different loves and thrown them off and others have tried my love and tossed me off. Nearly all have been good, and kind, or shallow but fun, and I have appreciated all of them, if only perhaps for a season, and they perhaps have appreciated me, and we are still friends, if still in touch. But they did not make me dream again: an excitement and simultaneous fear of loss that is gratifying and humbling.

I would like to travel, with and without you, and sail with and without you, and date you for those same years: a pleasure to spend a morning dancing like children to an old song while I make breakfast, and you make coffee in wide off-white potter's mugs with blue rims that say "all done" at the bottom.

I would like to do many things before we should ever call this anything. For when we touch the earth, we touch a foundation of interdependence and impermanence both: for we build this castle in the sky, in space. We are what stars or trees or streams are, and stars or trees or streams are what we are. And if things come together if only for a moment or an eon it is the same: it is a warrior's love song you and I can sing in the shower.

I would like to remember that you and I, we…began things properly. Slowly, deliberately, in the old way: as if we meant it.

A love story as maddeningly slow as the Japanese tea ceremony. Taking off our bamboo sandals, entering a tiny house, our robes cinched just-too tightly, our hair combed, our eyes clear, whisking the green thick tea, pouring spring water, my left hand shaking, your cheeks blushing.

Our getting to know one another has flowed through all available channels. We have been penpals; our courtship has been excitedly careful. Messaging on Facebook, Skyping, cell phone, an air visit to you, a road visit to me, a postcard on my refrigerator.

I would like to go for a walk with you in the Equinox rain through the old neighborhood with the noble houses and

~

spacious yards: I walk slowly and you walk quickly. I offer you my white woolen blue-striped sweater but the rain is light and cool, so it does not bother you. I am wearing a cowboy shirt. I would like to remember our early days, when we talked to one another but did not know one another: strangers, in love. Talking and laughing and sitting up straight and slumping and growing comfortable as ourselves with one another—all before sex seals something and intimacy is gained and space is lost, then regained.

Yes: I would like sex, I would like to fall in love, I would like to think ahead. But I would like to be here, now, even more, because here is where you are. I would like to begin things properly: for if I respect this match then I must begin things with the three kinds of confidence, without hesitation.

> *"So rouse that insight: be decisive, know what is, see clearly—these are the three kinds of confidence."*
> *~ Chögyam Trungpa, The Sadhana of Mahamudra.*

And so I would like to come in from the sea and I would like to see you every day, but not all day. I would like you to have space and be alone and then I would like to live our list: we can bicycle with Red dog along the bike path along the creek and we can climb, yoga, run together through those mountain foothills hit hard by the floods.

I do not know you, you worry, sometimes: *am I too bold, is this*

⌒

crazy? And that is a sane question, and I am glad you ask it. When it is dark and you have heard words of caution whispered in the wind from a friend who does not know me you question our course forward. Then I remind you in easy words that I am, only, me: I am not what you fear, your fear is what you fear, and I am something sillier, tougher—I am something more ordinary than what you fear. I am a basically good man, and I am happy to show my heart to your friends, and they are right to care for and protect you.

> *"Do not trust.*
> *If you trust you are in*
> *Others' hands.*
> *It is like the single yak*
> *That defeats the wolves.*
> *Herds panic and in trying to flee*
> *Are attacked.*
> *Remaining in solitude*
> *You can never be defeated.*
> *So do not trust,*
> *For trust is surrendering oneself.*
> *Never, never trust.*
>
> *But be friendly.*
> *By being friendly toward others*
> *You increase your non-trusting.*
> *The idea is to be independent,*
> *Not involved,*

~

Not glued, one might say, to others.
Thus one becomes ever more
Compassionate and friendly.
Whatever happens, stand on your own feet
and memorise this incantation:
'Do not trust.'" ~ Chögyam Trungpa

We are clan, and many proud warriors will sit up and smile their white teeth at the sound of my name.

The beginning of a love affair is like sending a single rickety rocket into the sky. You are right to be cautious: I am cautious. Walking into a love affair is akin to conducting a campaign of war. And I shall attack, parry, and laugh! For none of this is serious, none of this matters, but this matters to me, and this is serious to you. And so we may put our hearts into it and raise the warrior's cry as we bicycle through the tunnel, hollering from our *hara* so that the tunnel echoes this moment into another moment, or two—skipping a rock into time.

I would like to see you most every day for what I fear most is to miss seeing what you wear, how you laugh, and what you are creating, and what you think about things I think about, and what you think about things I have not thought about, and what you say out of that.

But: you may not complete me. You may not take me seriously, I may nourish your goodness. We may expand one another.

"A teacher can open the door, but you must enter by yourself." ~ Chinese proverb

I would like to see you arrive in my hometown from your home on the road: framed in my doorway, the sunshined white and green behind you, my maroon porch beneath you. I would like to undress your dress against the wall, wordlessly, and take you up, kissing your neck and kissing against your tangled hair, accidentally, and you hurriedly will move it aside. I would like to tangle your heart in mine and yet untangle them the next morning when, foggy, we drink coffee together in a cheerful café where men and women and children and dogs listen to four folks musicing in the wet sunshine. Our hair is messy, and Red dog is whining with excitement for the honeyed cookie baked in the shape of a dog bone that he knows I will buy for him. Seventy-five cents each, I'll buy two.

I would like to make fun plans with you, but then just do ordinary things; or plan ordinary things but find we have stepped through a wardrobe into a world of ordinary magic.

I would like to miss the farmers' market, nearly, because we are busy together. If we are late, we will get half price this and all the mixed greens you can fit in a bag for five dollars that or just fifty cents off a loaf of freshly baked walnut cranberry raisin bread and I will not mind either way because these are our people: farmers who make a living off of this land.

I would like to go to a yoga teacher who I recommend, with

~

you, and see her love you as she loves me, or go to the tamed kingdom in the mountains and visit the land I have known so well since I was a golden red-headed baby, and I would like to practice being here with you, so that we may be of better service.

I would like to go to hot springs with you, they are my favorite thing. And spend money that I have now to do nice things that then I was never able to do—I have always been stressed, working too much and loving it, poor yet wealthy in life and friendship. And finally though I am no longer poor, I am not yet wealthy in love.

I would like to read more of your handwriting, and go to wide parties with you, and admire you when you are unaware, and give you earrings made out of skateboards, and buy your art to gift to friends of mine, and I would like to see you find your home. I would like you to be relieved and breathe free because you find I am solid and stable and strong, which I am and have been and am more so now because of you.

Fire is surprising, for it comes from wood and other things.

There are many things I would like, but language constrains my desire into dreamlike forms. The great excitement of our love and fear of its loss has flooded our lives, but these words may guide such hope and fear into one channel, keeping our house dry but watering our garden nevertheless.

I would like to acknowledge that we cannot know the Future. But we are both kind and good people, who care about society, and prize open minds above opinions. And that is key. That and the basics: kissing, coffee, bicycling, flirting, art, and sun, and Red dog, and fruit and family and work and work, and work, and curious chaos. And, home.

And then I would like you to leave me and my heart will not know whether to be happy or sad at your visit or your departure.

Things I would like to do Rather than Fall for You.

"Meek means resting in a state of simplicity, being uncomplicated and, at the same time, approachable. Whether others are hostile or friendly, the warrior of meek extends a sense of kindness to himself and mercy to others. You are never seduced by trivial situations. Your awareness allows you to refrain from activities that dim the vision of the Great Eastern Sun.

You begin to see things as natural messages. You don't miss anything; you see every detail…the universe begins to become a part of you.

Tiger is basically experiencing a humble and gentle state of being.

Tiger expresses a combination of self-satisfaction and modesty…ambition and a poverty-stricken state of

~

mentality are overcome. You actually are able to jump into that vast and powerful ocean of magic…a natural sense of fulfillment which does not beg from others."
~ Chögyam Trungpa

I would like to say something like this:

There are so many human beings we meet, in this life.

I would like to find out which one you are. I cannot tell. Is it you?

I am not weak, but I am meek.

I am not one of the boys who pushes onto you with arrogance. I am better, different. You will have to meet me halfway. This is what a match is: tension in equality, a rhythmic balance, a sway that is not present if I am to dominate or be dominated. I would like neither. I would like a match.

You are not mine to take; I would not like to take you. You want to be taken; and so you are taken by another.

You wait: you give me an hour, once a moon, and when we commune beneath the cold light you hear something open.

Oh, yes.

Because I do not demand you, I do not get you.

I do not want something I can get out of you. I do not want something from you that I can take out of you. I would like to

～

share that which is freely and wholly given from your bedrock. Your longings, that are not a need but an echo off the rock, heavy beneath your waves.

I cannot view you as an object to be won or lost.

I would not like to keep you: a tiger must remain in the wild or it ceases to be Tiger. When we play, however, I would like to take you! I would like you to take me! I would like to ride you. We can take turns!

> *Padmasambhava, the Indian who first brought the Buddhadharma to high white Tibet, was said to ride a wild pregnant tigress. Ride not in any sexual sense, but in the sense of riding a powerful horse, or tiger in this case— riding the energy of the chaos of life, which takes guts and practice and skill. Together they worked to liberate the minds and hearts of all they encountered.*

And so we are in love but this is not yet Love.

I would like you to remember that if you are emboldened to hang a line up through time—if you open yourself for a month, or a week, or even a day, and stay with me, we will get to know one another.

I would like to begin to love you on a kitchen-sink level.

We could do dishes, and argue, and read, and hike, and grocery shop, and eat lunch by the creek, and I will not want to make love one night: "I'm tired." And you will not want to make

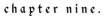

love in the morning: "I'm late to meet my friend." And we will text one another about small things: times and dates and funny photos. You could steal my toothpaste, and I could give you a new roll of toilet paper.

Love is in the details or it is not Love, after all.

I would like to see us know one another, instead of skimming the surface of Life until it runs out and we are nothing and all this is a fever dream, a cheap waste of this short, precious human life.

There are many ways to know one another. There are many ways to know if this is Love. I would like to lose at Scrabble against you. I would like to play volleyball with you. I would like to bicycle with you up the mountains.

Love is not about being the same. Love is about two humans appreciating one another. These are not pretty words—this is important. And if it is important, then we must laugh.

You are almost always cold; I am almost always warm. You like the blinds closed; I need the Sun to wake up. I like the windows open; you like to have two comforters and seven layers of old striped blankets (I counted), and me.

We will work it out: the windows will be open so I have my fresh air and breeze, and the heat will be low because I try to be an environmentalist but I will buy you warm slippers and make you tea and you can steal my big cardigans. And you will just have to get used to letting the Sun wake your sweet self up. You get all the blankets, I will fold them up over you and sleep with less.

You like your pancakes and bacon, you love fresh fish and good steak, I like pigs when they are alive—"they're smarter than dogs"—and for breakfast I like hippie stuff: organic granola and an organic banana and organic dark crunchy peanut butter in a glass jar and raw local honey and fresh-baked cinnamon raisin bread from a brown paper bag; we both love big salads with too many things in them like olives and artichoke hearts. We both like coffee in the morning, of course.

We will work it out, without compromising. But too we will each be the first to give an inch, many times over.

The key is not to take it personally, because I know your bedrock, and you know mine. The key is that you and I would like to be gentle more than we love to be right.

I would like to offer you a soft tee shirt to wear at night. I would like to take it off of you and lose it off the side of the bed and instead cuddle into our clean salt sweat.

I would like to talk with you, which includes listening and talking and not talking. I would like to do things together: go to another outdoor movie or eat vegan nachos with too much

~

hot sauce (but I keep one end of the plate free of hot, for you) and drink hoppy beer in another loud bright tap room or go on a road trip (you stick your long legs out the window, I eye your long legs) to go climbing together in a redpink canyon.

And I would like to not do things together, so that space in our daily lives gives us the air we require to handle love.

But you are afraid, or you are bold, or your desire is cool, or it is cautious, or your interest is shallow, or it is fast, or other boys distract you: and so I will raise a flag that shakes against the wind, light as the sun, for all to see.

But I will not earn your love, nor steal it: I will sing an old sad song and you will listen, or you will miss it.

> *Soooo you take the high rrroad…and I'll take the low… road…and I'll be in Scotland afore…yeee…for me and my true love…will never meet again, on the bonnie bonnie banks of Loch Loooomond.*

Take off your headphones when you bicycle: it is the most frustrating thing! I like you being alive and beautiful so much I shout for joy.

And I would like to dance with you, and see your low expectations in the face of your own childlike wonder raised up as high as my yellow flag. You deserve a good gentleman with a better hunger, and you deserve less of cowardly men's controlling desires and projections.

let's wear cowboy hats and nothing else.

And I would begin to love you truly, and if you love me too we will fall, fall, fall…fall like Alice into Wonderland. We will wake and stretch and brush our teeth and run Red dog around the park and shower quickly and then descend the spiral staircase in our shorts to the backyard hot tub beneath the good old tree. You will not be allowed in with make up. A light green leaf will fall in, and I will always rescue drowning bugs, and I will read a business book with water-wrinkled pages and wear a pale cowboy hat against the sun or rain, and you will read a good magazine until we are so hot, we hop out red-faced and sweating.

And you would wear bright lipstick occasionally—red with a hint of orange against your gold skin. And I would undress you, and you would undress me, and I would wait for you to scream through the walls before I took my turn: *such chivalry.*

chapter nine.

~

And I am already in love, but not merely with you. I am in love with what I see inside of your eyes: I can tell it is there for in the gaps of your midnight blue mind it flashes, like lightning! But you do not think you care about any of this: you are used to a cold world. You know the power of push, and I speak only the language of space.

But I do not mind being ignored: again I am not here to win, nor to get your attention, nor to get any thing. *I yam what I yam!* And though I may lose, too, it is your loss or victory, for I can no longer play games.

And so though I hold you up against the heroines of old…and though I respect the rock at the base of your being, I am not calculating. My humor burns orange: curl up against it and stretch out with a sigh and a yawn and curl up again and fall asleep. And in your dreams remember what your dreams already know: that Love is not weak, that desire based on connection burns hotter than desire based on conquest. I am not shy in my honesty, nor will you be in yours: I will overwhelm your hesitation, just as you could flood my life.

I would like to see you today. I miss doing the dishes with you, I miss grocery shopping with you, I miss laughing into you and being made fun of by you…I miss your hips, like a rocking chair.

I would like to meet you for more warmhotblackbrown in a heavy porcelain mug in a sunny-glassed café with old-fashioned dark wood paneling. And then I would stroll with you and Red dog up into the green, wet mountains, and then I would visit artists' homes with you, and see their work and care and precision, some of it brilliant, some of it dreamlike, some of it patient.

And I would like to invite you into my home again. And I would like to touch you: then and there, and soft but firmly and then more and, and you would not stop me, but your mouth would open with surprise but without sound.

I would like to do this one thing to you, not with you, just inside the entrance, feeling you rise against the doorframe. And then I would relax and let you do to me, too, not with me. And you might, again, kiss and breathe into my left ear, and I would laugh and growl into you like a friendly tiger: for I am ticklish. And you would press hard against the small of my back and though we started fast we would continue slowly, first on the wall, then the too-hard floor, then I would carry you, clumsily, for the stairs are narrow not wide. And you, and me, naked, simple, entwined: finally on my bed, under your many covers, shivering and then sweating. All within the space of an hour. And then, though it is still light evening, I would fall asleep against your breast. And you would wake me, it is dark evening now, and we would sink into the hot water in my old clawfoot bath, it needs to be re-lacquered. And I would like to read my book while you read your book, our arms intertwined as the steam rises and the bubbles settle.

And then, now, it is morning, and we would go up into the mountains and we would drive, and drive, and drive our way around the closed roads, still blocked by last month's

Morning!

unconditional flood of change. And we would dine together at the Nepali buffet, all you can eat for twelve bucks, first meal of the day.

I like the feeling of hunger for it reminds me of all those hundreds of months without you.

Missing you, thinking of you, like a friendly lonely thin tiger smelling the slip of a season into a new season.

If you and I spend our seasons together we would find that our dreams of happily-ever-after have holes in them through which the wind of karma blows: our yellow flag shakes.

And I would like you to look ahead and see what I know. The wind will replace our pretty ideas with something brighter: life.

We would schmooze (and shop) at the market. Later you would cook and I would like to help cut the carrots and we would dine with five candles and old music and I would like to do the dishes and you would dry and put them away. We would lean into big pillows and watch half an hour of a favorite movie that I am overly enthusiastic about before you fall asleep and I would get up and work for another hour and a half, until I fall asleep on the couch. And then you would wake early and leave me for a run, your hair shaking behind you. We would meet friends at their homes and have a good time, or a hard time. We would feel vulnerable in one another's presence, or forget one another and laugh into our drinks.

Do not worry. If you would like to make yourself safe from Love you could avoid our warmth by staying with an old boy who does not do you any good: he does not love you any, but sees you as a pretty possession that he is afraid to lose yet too arrogant to care for. Either way, he does not see your Nature: he sees you as Beauty. Or you could avoid our love by falling into life's vicissitudes: we are all so busy that it is easier to rush than to slow and be kind to ourselves! Can you see through your bright eyes that our quiet love is a rare thing, and if either of us is to treat its birth cavalierly, we do not deserve it? Can I slow and see or will I be too busy for us?

There is a positive arrogance in proclaiming that this, here, now is real and I acknowledge it against the tides of mediocrity: for our share of life is brightly finite.

This, here, now is real and I deserve she who deserves me and the world deserves two who will serve it with joy.

I see what you do not see, now: that your heart is a pearl polished into being by experience, rubbed together with caring as powerful as your ability to rest upon your rock, in reality, at this present moment, and to serve society with a positive arrogance that proclaims again: I have been given much and so, here I am.

I would like to see your pink art with witty black lines and frame it precisely and set it in shadows on a big, empty wall so that I might look into it as I look into your fire eyes, and be warmed in your absence.

I would like to ride my spotted horse while you ride your black horse and I would like to ride into the hills of my forefathers who own nothing.

I would like to hold your hand as it holds this green leaf, yellowed, that fell early from its tree, this Autumn. And I would like to imagine that it feels your careful care, for your eyes are warmed by your heart, and I would let you sadly nestle into me as a bird folds into its nest, resigning itself to a storm. For my heart is as large as a city, and it glows with a fire that, with the right mischievous love, shall serve to inspire thousands upon thousands to inspire thousands upon thousands.

Do not trust this friendly tiger: ride me.

It is easy.

"Tyger, tyger, burning bright

In the forests of the night,

What immortal hand or eye

Dare frame thy fearful symmetry?"

~ William Blake

chapter ten.

The Last Things I would like to Say to You.

"Never confuse a single defeat with a final defeat."
~ *F. Scott Fitzgerald*

These words are little moments of letting go.

And so I offer up this Letter to Cold, Old Girls of Winters' Past by dropping my memories into the fire and seeing what burns. Burning up of old provides oxygen for new.

We have not seen each other since that night when you wore pink pants, or that night where we sat up on the hillside and argued, pleasantly.

We never said good-bye—we simply never said hello again.

There are things you should know, things you should hear. You do not care to hear them but I offer them to you, anyway.

~

I cannot ask you to listen (talking to you is rainwater falling into an upside-down bowl, my offering is without expectation).

You are gone to me as I am gone to you.

But I do care for the memory of our courtship, and your cold heart that appeared like a skittish, lost dog.

And so I would say a few things…and tuck this hollow letter into an empty bottle and cork it, and set the bottle adrift beneath the pier. And perhaps it will find its way to Cow City, or Old Harbor City, or West Ocean City, or Gray Skyscraper City, or Fog City, or a distant island or perhaps it will be lost across the ocean.

I would like to have said these things…so that you cease hurting kind men and stop allowing yourself to be pushed upon by bully men.

"Beauty is only skin deep, but ugly goes clean to the bone." ~ Dorothy Parker

I would like to have said these things:

I would like to say that your beauty made it difficult to breathe.

I would like to remember the sound of your call: but only for a moment, for you are a siren, and I have much sailing left to do.

I would like to say that I do not mind not being friends with you, now, for what is left to me is the memory of you and our good, bad dates and our bad whiskey and our wild, fun, sexual, drunken dancing together. I would have kissed you that night but your acrid mouth smelled of put-out cigarette butts. I remember your thong, you against the wall, you on my bed on all fours, your wide open eyes, narrowing, your bangs…my temporary humor and your model ice melting in the hands of memory as a frozen polaroid, perfect as the Autumn leaves veined in red and lit-up orange.

And then they fall, dry, we are over. The end.

You are a once-bright yellowgreen leaf! But your season is turning. You have sold your self to hungry men who will touch every part of you except your cynical heart.

"There are only the pursued, the pursuing, the busy and the tired." ~ F. Scott Fitzgerald

Your leaves are now beige fodder for future seasons.

You will soon be rolling a vast baby carriage into a café and eyeing the young party girls with wistful condescension. Your thick husband will be distant and have affairs. And so will you. You will visit a doctor when you are not sick, to fake your self back to a fake perfection.

I would like to say that you were cruel to me, and many others, because you could be. You knew the power you possessed and you did not use your power for good: oh if you had you could have raised waves against the cruel tides of suffering. Instead you used it as a fix for your boredom; you used it to drown out your own humanity, your beautiful loneliness, your sweet insecurity, your kind fear.

But your power could not hold me for long. I was not interested in *having* you: your carefully delicious style, your elfin eyes, your breasts, your hair, your fit arms, your strong neck, your butt, your gold shoulders, your gold legs, your too many bangles.

Those things were like chimes to my ears, a call that sounded across the waters and riveted my attention. Riveting like… like a duplicitous chorus. I was not long blinded by your brilliance: I kept looking into you, and as I looked, you softened.

> *"All that grace, all that body, all that face, makes me want to party…will you still love me when I'm no longer young and beautiful? Will you still love me when I've got nothing but my aching soul?"*
> *~ Lana del Rey, The Great Gatsby.*

And as you softened…you made a poor choice. You played cold games with me—you treated me as you had treated the others.

But you did not think of this: it takes two to play and I would not play your cold games with you. And so you lost me.

And you did not care.

But it is our loss, nevertheless.

> **"'Does it hurt?' asked the Rabbit.**
> **'Sometimes,' said the Skin Horse, for he was always**
> **truthful. 'When you are Real you don't mind being hurt.**
> **…but these things don't matter at all, because once**
> **you are Real you can't be ugly, except to people who**
> **don't understand.'"**
> **~ Margery Williams, The Velveteen Rabbit.**

My cold games are fun: they involve wool, and snow! Snowshoeing with Red dog and seven other dogs and friends and hot chocolate afterward; or sledding down the mountain foothills where our elders used to ski, or rolling a snowball until it weighs more than two men; or baseball tossing snowballs at snowheavied trees to relieve their aching branches.

Your cold games are something out of a girl's heavy fashion magazine: they smell of sweetly toxic perfume samples.

I thought I knew you: and I still believe that you are better than this. You just have not had the encouragement.

But I respected myself: I was too patient, and strong in my broken places (*shinjang*), and I was lucky enough to have been encouraged by kind warriors. So I was not desperate for something that did not care for itself.

I *was* desperate for your honesty, for your hasty laughter, for your gentle breath, for your inspiring coos over my shoulder, for your dry tears, for your ordinary friendship.

I do miss your cozying into my gray couch in the Winter beneath a black-striped red wool blanket when I brought you tea and you continued reading my used book to me. There was such promise in our Winter. I sat beneath you on the maroon carpet and fed the fireplace. I was not desperate for your attention, but rather your *caring*—you were afraid of love, for desperate boys had lobbed it up at you all of your externally beautiful life.

And so you sought after troubled boys who did not love.

And so I let you go and so I relax my pursed lips and close my tired eyes and listen to Red dog sigh and mutter in his sleep. I jump into bed, warming the cool spots with my long strong legs. I try to read but my eyes are tired. I dream dreams of service that I can blow air into, and make real. My aching chest wounded, pinned beneath me.

And so I would like to thank you. You taught me, again and again, again and again and again, not to dream of you. Finally I listened. I am silent. These words are not words of love, but of the silence that remains when this letter is done. I have listened and I do not continue to imagine our love, for it was not love. You were too busy walking your red carpet, and it was my misstep that I thought we had something more than an hour's fun.

And I would remind you: I was never one of your fans.

> **"It is impossible to live without failing at something, unless you live so cautiously that you might as well not have lived at all—in which case, you fail by default."**
> ~ *J.K. Rowling*

Thank you, for clarifying for me what love is not.

Love is no thing, and nothing is a gift, space is a playground, and time and distance are merely cold peaks and green valleys in the topography of genuine love.

For I know what I deserve: one who is not afraid of her heart. Love does not require a map: it makes its way across the miles. Love does not heed the time; it does not care for one or two moons. Love is not bothered by obstacles—they form the high sides to the left and right of this rocky path. This path does not depend upon external signs: love will find its own way.

And my love will wait, a tiger in the tall grass, and my love will relax and curl up then stretch out and nap and sigh. And you will be there, but it will not be you, it will be Her: I cannot tell who she will be and this is not for me to know.

I am here.

> **"I miss you like hell."** ~ *Edna St. Vincent Millay*

chapter eleven.

Things I would like to do this Cold Season without You.

"There is a pleasure in the pathless woods;

There is a rapture on the lonely shore;

There is society where none intrudes,

By the deep sea, and the music in its roar:

I love not man the less, but Nature more…"

~ Lord Byron

In the wake of your vanishing from my country a season has taken hold, and another will soon take its place. Halloween, Thanksgiving, Christmas, New Year's Eve.

I would like to miss you, when I think of you.

I would like to feel sad, and bitter, and that angst shall warm my hollowed-out heart as this season grows colder.

What a life I lead, where you for whom I feel something like the fire that burns in the heart of love walks boldly into my living room and tells my friends of your love for another. And my guests applaud, not knowing of my feelings. And I retreat upstairs to the sound of my breaking heart, cracking further. I have been stupid to feel—I get the message, you could not put it more clearly.

I will not join the birds in their whistling outside your faraway sunny window, tomorrow morning.

I would like to grow a little cold inside: not so cold that beautiful ice with patterns in it has begun to form around the edges, not Winter's cold—not yet. Just wet, damp, the kind of increasing Fall cold that sneaks up into the heart and chills it. And I would like a second blanket, and my handmedown maroon Pendleton sweater, and tea in a big mug I made myself.

～

But the morning comes.

My home routine is boring, and it is good.

Hot sun wakes me in my wide bed. I brush my teeth. Red dog and I stumble out into the new day: he wanders the pocket park behind my tall house doing his stuff while I hang from an old orchard tree and do a few pull-ups and stretch. I avoid looking at my phone. If it is hot out I walk him further, to a century-old farmer's ditch to swim. Back home, I order him to lie down while I dish his raw food out. *Okay!* He eats hurriedly: it is the highlight

the New New Yorker? ...

~ *See you in 2 hours.*

of his day, every day. I meditate: dedicating the merit of this day to others, then read a few paragraphs of *Training the Mind*. Red dog lies by my side. I walk down my maroon spiral staircase to the hot tub where I read *The New Yorker* or a business book (if it is bright out, or snowing, I wear a cowboy hat to shield my eyes). Dripping, I wind back up the twirly staircase to the clawfoot tub where I shower, soaping off hot sweat while singing Brave Wolfe or Drunken Sailor or Dona, Dona or Loch Lomond through bubbles. After showering, I wrap my self in a towel and dry in the echoes of the sun on my balcony where, each day, I can

~

see the mountains a little more, again: the leaves are all falling.

And though this now early Autumn sun is still hot…my skin and hair are wet and soon I am goosebumped. Red dog stands, shakes, walks from sunny patch to shade. In an hour his busy itinerary will call for him to stand, shake, and walk to a sunny patch. I dress in confident clothes. Downstairs, I toast cinnamon raisin bread—my favorite. My kitchen suddenly smells as if I bake. I bicycle to a favorite café and work on my laptop and socialize all day, getting so much done yet never enough. Things are going well: my business is a bonfire on a beach patiently built up, bigger and bigger with little twigs for twelve years.

~

This is how I am without you, now.

I stand in my kitchen, leaning against the sink,
for an hour, my eyes seeing memories.

You are gone—

I have not lost you, however.

You are not one of a long line of those I have given up,

for I never could have you.

The beginnings of Love had me.

My sullen heart

was had, yet again.

~

You are lost to me:

safe in your City,

safe in your Country,

safe with another Heart,

safe on the other end of your Phone Number.

…and now I would like to go to a cold cabin alone up on a hill above a stream and pretend to be old.

It will soon be cold but not yet freezing. I do not think well, anymore. I do not think of anything, much: I am too full of conditional feeling. The feeling we call sadness.

Soon I would like to hide my face behind a red beard, it has already started, and the red sideburns will curl as they are wont to do. I will wear a red hat over my matted hair.

And when I bicycle back down to this twinkling town, this white Winter, I would like to go to bars alone and laugh thickly and convince random friends of friends of my joy. I would like to enjoy fun too fully without pausing to savor it, like an emptied glass against another night. This is the time when sorry men drown in drink, but I like to sip good scotch, and in the morning an Americano. Both are the color of lacquered wood and both taste like a kiss—a brief moment of dreams. They are all like this: "There you go, you are happy, you are popular…" They will think of me no more. They do not care. I am a favorite old café that people like to frequent, but if I close, folks mutter and move on.

And yes this is all you have been to my sadness. A match for me to burn myself up again.

And now I have that much less hope and that much less fear.

This is good—this season of increasing cold.

A moment of truth and caring and a soft moment when my life opened like a frightened fucking flower as my heart felt fire and then, gone, like the scotch. So I order another, and lean against the bar and I do not watch my friends of friends lean against one another in love.

And I do not pity my sadness, for it is my friend and I do not pity my friends.

I cannot run from our encounter, for it is too late to run. I can already feel the red circle growing beneath my jacket and my sweater, staining my wrinkled cotton dress shirt. I can feel the warm blood, my chest shot through with Cupid's arrow.

I would not like to blame you: you briefly gave my days so much and I thank you for opening me.

I would like to have worn armor, but I did not: it weighs me down on the battlefield. You would have liked it if I had worn armor, so you could joust at my heart longer: a foolish red heart deflated by a callous, careless cut. Instead I wore a robe, and I tied on two swords—one of them this pen—and for a time I dazzled you with my skill as I gazed at the reflection of your

～

face in the stream. But you did not want my heart: you wanted to read my words, and go home with steel.

> **"...They smashed up things and creatures and then retreated back into their money or their vast carelessness, or whatever it was that kept them together, and let other people clean up the mess they had made."**
> **~ F. Scott Fitzgerald**

My hope lied, my fear gone cold. Perhaps I will reawaken next Spring or the Spring after that. Perhaps I will never flower for another? In any case I live on, and on, and on, and...and it is Winter that is coming soon.

I would like to wear the armor of my red Mountain and green Forest clans against this white Winter: I like thick wool redwarm shirts. I would like to find such an old shirt and buy it, or buy it new now in a small shop where it was delivered from a brick warehouse in an old town in this young country where it was made in the old way. And I would like to wear a grandfather's cardigan with a big collar to keep my neck warm. I would like to wear tweed over that, I would like to wear dark jeans every day, and buck wingtips, and drink tea out of a big glass jar.

And soon I will go to the cabin in the white Forest above the stream below the Mountain.

And when it is warmer, next Spring, I will go to the troubled

Holy Land, and to All Light or All Dark City, and to the Red Roof City, and perhaps to the capitol of my country, but not to my mother's country. My mother will visit my mountain valley for my birthday.

And when it is warmer, next Summer, I would like to invite my beautiful friends to take their clothes off but keep some on, and we will spend all day at the swimming hole.

But all of this is so far away. And so for now we will pick our favorite pumpkin and bicycle up and down hills and layer up and layer down and we are all so busy, there is no room for love, but it happens anyway when you sit in a café and look at the lengthening shadows against the sunny wall across the street. And we will find a copper bar that serves food and do our work in there, nights, and bike home over the snow.

I would like to have loved you, but I never found your rock bottom. You never let me.

"Suzanne takes you down

to her place near the river

You can hear the boats go by

You can spend the night beside her

And you know that she's half crazy

But that's why you want to be there

And she feeds you tea and oranges

That come all the way from China

And just when you mean to tell her

That you have no love to give her

Then she gets you on her wavelength

And she lets the river answer

That you've always been her lover…"

~ Leonard Cohen

Things I would like to do
After our Fall.

*"He found himself wondering at times, especially in the
autumn, about the wild lands, and strange visions of
mountains that he had never seen came into his dreams."*
~ J.R.R. Tolkien

In the days and months in future present moments when I
remember you, I would like to remember that you were always
lost to me.

I would like to see that you showed me a view through a window
that was opened, but we never climbed outside to play in the tall
grass. And even later when I showed you my home, and you
talked with Red dog, well: that was all there was for us.

And then you left and our two lives unraveled: I went this way
and you went that way, our dreams no longer entwined.

~

And I kept my horses reined in, and they did not mind, for they share my proud spirit, and they feel sure that some day soon I shall let them run.

But even without our dreams I would like to remember your hair and eyes and stripes and the golden things that we did together. And most of all your kind command. I would like to see you revolving a world even if it is not mine.

And it was one of our only evenings: seven, eight…not more than eleven or fourteen or fifteen in all. I would like to recall how I was tired, walking across the bridge over the roaring white river in the night.

I would like to think upon the future, and build a path toward it. I would like to be a father to trouble-making children, and I would like to be a husband to a mother and a lover whom I am always grinning after. And first, I would like to date, and first I would like to travel the world! A red line tracing my many new adventures. But I have explained all this, and the words are without object: this heart has only itself left to feel affection for—for now.

And the Small Town with the two streets and the fanciful old houses and the slow river and the endless woods: I shall return to the Forest, and leave the City behind.

I would like to remember that you look just as good with your girlfriends and boyfriends at a house party as you do when dressed for a conference, in a hotel, in black heels too high.

You mined my depths, and you found space many fathoms deep, and you kept drilling, and you hit bedrock, but you wanted oil.

The beauty of Autumn is that things in their dying change, and the beauty in this change is the reminder that life is short. Appreciate the passing. The bright leaf and green beauty of Summer and now yellow Fall has sent you, and me—us—and our budded, blossomed love off and away on a random breeze. And now my pen's black words are shown for what they are: powerless against the revolution of the season.

I was sleepy with good hot tea and you and I sitting on the worn Persian rug and in those moments I lost you. Any breeze can take an entire future away from any one of us.

I would like to return to my work.

I would like to tell my friends *no*. I would like to bicycle the roads alone. I would like to suit up and get coffee for-here in a small thick off-white porcelain cup and drink the shot and ride, off, long…and in a week or two my beard will have come in and I will be warmly bitter against the cold. I will begin dating again: a way of life that is fun, busy, a sport. But I miss

chapter twelve.

~

you: the possibility of being interested in the other end of a conversation. I will miss your shy hair and impossibly wide eyes and your stripes and the promise: that, perhaps, I could find a friend to want to love me.

> *"I'm offering a lot, I'm offering me." ~ Joanne Woodward, to Paul Newman in A Long, Hot Summer.*

Me.

That word encompasses my affections, my childhood, my future accomplishments, my ups, my downs, my victories, my accidents, my lost things, my forgotten adventures. Together, me and she (who remains unknown)—we will enjoy many succinct times where friendship gilds daily life.

This is our dance.

I reached out, sweetly, with confidence

You assented, with a shy smile

I stepped forward again, straightforward

You invited me in

We fell into step with one another, a coming together.

Then, you slowed me down and pushed me away

~

and I stepped back.

And then you called to me, not to leave and

I listened and stepped forward

and then you pushed me away and called to me simultaneously so I offered space,

And then you stopped me from leaving and came to me

And I returned to your fold and we came together, again

And then you pushed me away a fifth time,

And I was done, and you were offended at my displeasure,

And I let you drop.

chapter thirteen.

Things I would like to do Before I Return.

"Happiness makes up in height for what it lacks in length." ~ Robert Frost

When I lose at love, I do not lose love itself—but rather one possibility of love. So I pause—I turn from my past and commit myself to this new now—to the hard and worthwhile work of making friends with myself.

Then, I pause again—and dive forward into an unknown future, with elation ballooning my heart.

"Always fall in with what you're asked to accept.
Take what is given, and make it over your way.
My aim in life has always been to hold my own with
whatever's going. Not against: with." ~ Robert Frost

chapter thirteen.

~

You and I have not met our Futures yet.

I said good-bye to my Future with you; I turned and looked into the old fireplace mantle mirror, and at myself, and then through myself—but I cannot see my Future.

I would like you to know that though we loved brightly (and I should therefore be sad to have lost us), I was only sad briefly.

For I have lost a Future we did not, after all, wish to win.

Rather, I would like to thank you. I am grateful to have loved again, a little—my heart had gone quiet for too long.

> *"What happened to the old bank? It was beautiful."*
>
> *"People kept robbing it."*
>
> *"Small price to pay for beauty." ~ Butch Cassidy*

The Future, she is not here yet.

I would like to find her name on The List. And so I date and date and date and date and date…and I am alone and alone and alone and alone and alone…furthering this difficult yet satisfying friendship with myself.

But now it is Now, the Summer it is past and the Spring has not yet come: our Past is done, and my Future? She *will* come.

~

"The mountains are calling and I must go." ~ John Muir

I would like to close up my yellow house, this weekend.

I would like to retreat away, up into the mountains where whiskey Autumn is all falling into white Winter. I would like to bicycle, towing Red dog (in a dog coat, in a bicycle trailer). Red dog would like to run, it is more fun—but it is eleven miles out of my Small City and up into the cold Wooded Mountains so he will spend most of his time in the trailer.

I would like to bicycle up—up, calmly, up, slowly, up, my breath visible, up—puffing rhythmically like an old steam train. The high roads may be frozen in spots, it is early morning: the trick is to keep the black tires straight, and when I turn, to turn gradually.

I would like to bicycle past pale farms and up, up between the cold mountains until I get to the half-frozen noisy black river where I turn at my red dirt road, dusted white with snow. I would like to open the rust-polished wide gate. I let Red dog off his leash and he runs with a yelp of joy. Together we climb up to my closed-up cabin in the dark woods.

I would like to open up my cabin. This is where we first fell in love. It is cold, now.

I would like to spend my first hour moving good dried wood inside and chopping new wood, blushing, flushed with sweat. Deep breaths in, and visible air out. The sun is setting.

~

I would like to light the cold fireplace. I set the dusty copper kettle out to make tea, and take off my sweaty clothes, and put on my warm red-black checkered union suit pajamas. I would like to spend the night reading the *Collected Short Stories* beneath many heavy warm blankets. I would like to begin with *The Rich Boy*, again.

I would like to not eat: now is a time for retreat, for brief asceticism, for rest—a time for alone, a time to make my acute sadness hungry and draw it out, and to sit with it at my barren kitchen table. But I would like to take care of myself, too: I packed a brown paper bag of almonds, and another bag of figs, and the makings for oatmeal each morning and lentil soup I will heat over the fire at night. There is brown sugar in the cupboard.

> *"Experiencing the upliftedness of the world is a joyous situation, but it also brings sadness. It is like falling in love. When you are in love, being with your lover is both delightful and very painful. You feel both joy and sorrow. That is not a problem; in fact, it is wonderful.*
>
> *It is the ideal human emotion.*
>
> *The warrior who experiences windhorse feels the joy and sorrow of love in everything he does.*
> *He feels hot and cold, sweet and sour, simultaneously. Whether things go well or things go badly, whether there is success or failure, he feels sad and delighted at once."*
> *~ Chögyam Trungpa*

~

I would like to be alone, so that I can relax, so that I can cry if I am lucky.

If I cry I would like to smile simultaneously: water together with sunshine produces rainbow.

As I am brokenhearted, I must remain cheerful where self-pity would otherwise lie. Alone, my exposed heart is safe to feel full of appreciation, even joy. Alone, I can relax into tender pain.

As I let go of our Future, it is already gone.

~

My small cabin's small bed is solid, built against a small window. Before I go to sleep, I would like to open the window at my head, though it is cold out: just a crack, so that when I sleep beneath my many wool blankets I can breathe innocent air. Air allows for space, gives wisdom and blessing to those of us who would guard space, and lends love to those of us who need space.

The window faces East, so that each morning's first light pours over me.

> *"My sorrow, when she's here with me, thinks these dark days of autumn rain are beautiful as days can be; she loves the bare, the withered tree; she walks the sodden pasture lane." ~ Robert Frost*

Oh, you had messaged me. You told me I was too much, and you were right: I was too much for us.

For I know I am too much, and that is not too much. So I am not defeated. Rather I have lost something that was not enough: you did not want what I have to offer, which is all of me. If I am not what you would like you cannot be what I would like and so I cannot let go of us—we are already gone.

Now, when I would like to think of us—I see only gray ghosts in the mirror.

I grow this red beard until it curls. This beard is good for mourning, and for bicycling in the Winter.

I would like to appreciate our time together: joyful, picnic, patience, *The New Yorker* in the hot tub, sex, laughter, listening, forest beach, orange lipstick, sweet voice, your wide curving eyes,

~

postcards, mosquitoes and sharing—and all of it in a season.

And I would like to thank you—even as the wide, white fog rises up the mountain hills around and below my cabin retreat.

I would like to say, as a wise man liked to do, *Jolly Good Luck, sweetheart!*

I would like to add, as I wave good-bye, *Thank you for being you, just you.*

"No spring nor summer beauty hath such grace as I have seen in one autumnal face." ~ John Donne

This Winter will be long but this end of Autumn feels endless.

Alone, I do things and focus upon doing them fully. Tea, a walk in the forest with Red dog, reading a book…I turn from distraction to what is happening. Mourning is my meditation.

And so before turning to future Her I honor past you.

I do not need to let go…time has already left us behind…I need merely to ready myself to once again step into the flow of the already rushing river.

I would like to turn, and take a dance step forward now—without you! My feet are hesitant, but confident, too. I would like to turn my gaze away from our Summer love affair and toward my Winter, alone, away from Green Mountains and toward Red Mountains—to the fog clinging to our foothills below.

So, though I have lost our Future, I am patient with my mourning so that I may open, once again, to another.

I would like to see what comes to me, and I would like to choose whether to swing at the pitches I see.

"Everybody needs beauty…places to play in and pray in where nature may heal and cheer and give strength to the body and soul alike." ~ John Muir

I would like to look forward to other lovers, but I cannot yet move my mind through this mountain fog. There are gray ghosts in the white fog: and my red beard is not all grown in yet.

So I move my body, instead: I take my old climbing rope leash and put on my light running shoes and my gray short shorts and "C'mon, Red dog!" He whines with excitement as we begin to jog around and up the mountain. For the future does not long wait before becoming now and I must run to higher ground to leave your fog behind.

I return in a salt sweat three hours later and the cabin is dusty and empty but warm.

I have been here for a day or two, then three days. I would like to stay for thirty more days, or ninety.

So, though I would like to stow my steel bicycle inside, and batten down for the Winter, I will not. For this long bicycle ride up into these flood-ripped mountains must be a round-trip journey. My Small City flickers back up at me. And so my bike stays outside, leaning against the cabin wall, not too well-sheltered beneath the old rippling tin porch awning.

But for today, this retreat in the Mountains is a white and dark green delight.

The cool air pushing up against and through my tweed and cotton is a delight.

When waking in the cabin, or after running, or while writing: drinking water or coffee or whiskey is a delight.

Today, I find new love in old things: I am a child, once again captivated for minutes by the forest, the light, the occasional mountain snow, the wind, the wood, sounds—in love with the details of this natural world and this human life.

Gnomes still live in the old forests, according to this silly book I read when I was a boy. Short, strong, jolly, horny, hungry, with white beards or rosey cheeks and tools and warm homes beneath trees.

Are there still spirits here? I do not know.

The deer know the weather. The green leaves are gone the gold leaves are gone the faded dry crumbling leaves are gone. Last night the winds took the leaves away and now, suddenly: barren,

~

gray, and white. Our world is ready for more Winter.

I would like to be still, and listen to the subtle sounds of the woods. Listening relaxes the City out of me.

I would like to know how the animals and their hungry children live amongst the red barked pine trees sweet with sap when the cold snow comes and does not leave.

~

I cry: I am alone, and it is dark, and it is water into water when I spend an evening hour in the old white bathtub outside. Two years ago I set it on a slope, built it up on top of heavy rocks with room below for an old black woodstove that I bought at a mining town yardsale. I have spent evenings bathing laughing and making love with a friend, too hot, looking at the crisp stars, drinking cold hoppy beer, then letting the cooled water drain out when we are done.

Now I am alone, with my ghost memories and new space, salt tears merging with salt sweat. Patience is a recipe for purification: juniper gin, the salt and sweat and hot water, night stars, the moon, cutting fragrant wood and smoke, reading, running, doing nothing, listening, dreaming, waking.

In my tears I remember your strongsoft body with silk blouse waving open in vague wrinkles. You are stretched before me, your mind rich with cozy second-floor cafés with poetry readings and dear friends and beeswax candles and debates about war with meaningful laughter and meals along long

⌒

tables with photos of placesettings taken from above, just so, and lovers and more lovers and textbooks and paper-books and houseparties in hallways and new-old music and carryon-only travel and kissings in beds. Joy and desire, humor and dance. In my tears you are walking step by step back and away from me, receding.

Looking backward is as if looking at a shadow, or a movie: after awhile, we long for real! And so I would like to look forward, but the Future is not yet alive, and though Now is pregnant with it, all I have is Now. So I walk mindfully up the forest path, today.

In the Future I will jump into a waterhole on a hot day and skip rocks and ropeswing up, let go, splash, the cool water washing my hair back, blinking wetblur out of my eyes as we wade in water with dogs chasing tennis balls.

But for now I am alone in a cabin in a forest on a mountain, with countrybright stars reflecting at my unloved orange eyes.

> **"When I run through the deep dark forest long after this begun**
>
> **Where the sun would set, trees were dead and the rivers were none**
>
> **And I hope for a trace to lead me back home from this place…" ~ First Aid Kit**

This morning for the first time the fog has cleared and I can see the little gold lights below, and I remember that late Fall in my Big Town is a bright and blue delight.

This morning for the first time I would like to return to my Small City.

A weekend retreat is a quick recipe for renewal.

Things I would like to Let Go of Before I See You.

"Feelings like disappointment, embarrassment, irritation, resentment, anger, jealousy, and fear, instead of being bad news, are actually very clear moments that teach us where it is that we're holding back. They teach us to perk up and lean in when we feel we'd rather collapse and back away. They're like messengers that show us, with terrifying clarity, exactly where we're stuck.

This very moment is the perfect teacher, and, lucky for us, it's with us wherever we are." ~ Pema Chödrön

After a day and then another away from my Small City, having taken refuge up high in these mountains…I would still like to stay still, alone and hidden for another lifetime.

But I would not like this, really, for life and chaos and fear wake my heart—just as strong coffee enlivens the blood in one's veins. And so, shivering, I jump out of bed and pull on my longsleeve handmedown wool shirt and long underwear and thick graywhite socks and heavy, stiff dark jeans and a grandpa cardigan sweater with high collar and a secondhand tweed jacket with leather-braided buttons and wornsmooth elbow patches, and black bike shoes, and a khaki knit hat and fingerless gloves.

And I roll back down the road across the river through the polished rust gate and down, down, down with Red dog in the trailer behind my bike—back to life.

warm
socks
cold
nights
~

~

Back to the distant Small City, for I am eager to make trouble.

After only nearly three days, in retreat, riding my sadness out, I found my buried red heart and washed it clean in the black river. And I have found that it is still full of humor, and forward-movement, and commonsense, and head-shaking rhythm, and charm and listening: *power*.

I am back in my Tall House on a Long Hill in my Big Town beneath the Red Mountains above the Great, Golden Plains.

And I would like to ask one out and stroll with her past old houses with screened-in porches; and I would like to ask two out and watch half of an old movie by E.M. Forster, and she would like to lie on her tummy as I hold her; and I would like to ask three out, but she will have a boyfriend; and I would like to ask four out, and she will not reply; and I would like to ask five out and we will climb and sit on red rocks in the blue wind; and I would like most of all to wait and look for one who would like to look through my orange eyes to where the water is clear.

In the meantime, dating is a wonderful waste.

"Sometimes, though, he would have a cocktail in the bar, and he told me about the girl in the red tam, and his adventures with her, making them all bizarre and amusing, as he had a way of doing, and I was glad that he was himself again, or at least the self that I knew, and with which I felt at home. I don't think he was ever

143.

*happy unless some one was in love with him, responding
to him like filings to a magnet, helping him to explain
himself, promising him something. What it was I do
not know. Perhaps they promised that there would
always be women in the world who would spend their
brightest, freshest, rarest hours to nurse and protect that
superiority he cherished in his heart."*
~ F. Scott Fitzgerald, The Rich Boy.

Finally, one day after I meet you I would like to ask you out on a date, and you would like to go, and you will like me and I will like you, and it will become clear that She out there is you right here.

In the beginning I will not know that She is you.

And you will not know He is me.

I would like to find you when I do not expect Her, and ask you out right away, before we have to wait for the Future. I will ask you to your face, with a grin. And though today is hot and quiet I do not feel irritated or cold: I enjoy this life.

I would sometimes like our Future to be here Now. She and He living a country life together: planning little, resting, playing, swimming, working, cooking, going to a few things with friends. I would like to walk in the already-cold early evening on top of light white snow and wet yellow leaves and you could make me feel all better or I could make you feel all better or we could talk about work or ethics. I would like to never stop trying to get you to laugh.

But it is not yet that day—so I must make my own luck.

But now I am alone for it is still a Then that we will look back upon. Alone is a thing without melody. It is, rather, a sweet thing, a sharp, riveting thing, a polished thing. Alone is a succinct thing worthy of a single taut sentence. Alone is a chaotic thing worthy of long sentences: sentences that reluctantly ebb and flow, feint and flourish, rise and plunge and only close when they are most open—like other lovers too hot for the top sheet.

Alone? It is perfect for this Fall.

It is Fall and each morning (I wake), each morning I step out on the balcony of my tall house and stretch and,

Good morning, sunshine!

…I bellow, as we did when young at Camp. Everyone smoked too much and drank "borrowed" vodka in the woods and kissed too hard and laid around in grass, lots, and golden-browned marshmallows on campfires and I was often lonely and often cheerful and often genuine and always living my life in the first draft.

Each morning now is bright for the Past, cold at Present, sharp with the Future: each morning leaves so many memories forgotten.

~

"In three words
I can sum up everything
I've learned about life:
it goes on."
~ Robert Frost

The newly fallen leaves: they were just green this Summer! Each one a colorfully enthusiastic masterpiece of life, beauty, and now loss. Summer is gone fast as I grow up, it used to be wonderfully empty and endless but now it is full and too quick.

Bicycling through tunnels I *whoop!* My echo reminds my sadness to be brave. I bicycle past dry fields and over bumpy trails and over wooden *ratatatatat* bridges and on the shoulders of busy roads where cars and trucks *whoosh* past me, the drivers texting friends, practicing un-meditation: practicing wishing they were somewhere else.

I would like to think that I am ready for you—ready as I have ever been. I am finally able to take the time to travel; or settle down; or both. I have the money to buy a plane ticket or a dinner without fearing that my card might b-bounce. I would like to see you for lunch on the lawn at farmers' market, tomorrow—it is one of the last of the season.

And I would like to be sad: this sadness is good. When you are sad, remember this: sing old warriors' songs.

Sing blues. Sing in the shower.

The Minstrel Boy to the war has gone!

In the ranks of death you will find him

His father's sword he has girded on!

His wild harp slung behind him

Awake! Awake! Is the warrior's cry

The world, the world deceeeeeives thee…

These songs are sung by the pure and free!

They'll never sound in slav'ry.

Things I would like to do with You when I am Drunk.

"Happiness consists in realizing it is all a great strange dream." ~ *Jack Kerouac*

There is a small pine wreath in your dark hair.

I am a big man, I can handle five drinks in a row, or six, or seven. I just light up like a wax wrapper, lit on fire. I can still walk straight and dance and talk and laugh and make jokes that make others laugh. And then you come in, an hour after I have been there, bored, and I did not think you were coming.

You are tall and beautiful and wearing white. I do not know you, and you do not know me, but we have enjoyed one another's company, recently, a bit—talking and laughing. You are clearly intelligent, tasteful, and apparently, you tell me now, you are young. I had no idea: your taste, conversation, ambitions and laughter are all beautiful and formed, not raw or messy or wild,

149.

~

but composed, like an exquisite photograph.

We talk and laugh and eat and drink and toast and talk with others and do our things. It is a party. And we talk with old people and I flirt at you and you listen to the toasts from people you do not know to others you do not know, much, which is sweet—because these are special moments for people I love.

At the end of our night I would like to walk you to your car, but I run into someone, I do not remember—and you wait a bit, which is sweet. And we walk and talk and are frank but respectful. I hate being respectful, women do not find it attractive, but I care more for my own conscience and integrity than kissing a woman when it is not time.

And I guess you are engrossed in our snowy walk and talk, for we walk ten blocks out of the way, and there is a moment, where we turn to reverse course, with the snow and the yellow light in the night when it is time to kiss you! But I do not dive into the moment. Perhaps I should have, but I would rather make love with a beauty than chase a kiss. Making love is passion plus heart, and I would not have one without the other.

And so I would like to keep walking with you in the snow and when we say *good-bye*—you are driving home to your family for Christmas across the white Plains—I remind you to respect my respectfulness of you, for nice guys do always lose, and I am nice, but I do not always lose.

Christmas is for parties, and celebrations, and family amongst strangers, and for remembering how short and sweet life is, and for being cozy, and for long drives across the white Plains. And you are gone, now, and I am set for another good day of work and play: hike with Red dog and a friend and her dog, hot chocolate-colored coffee, work on my laptop, hot tub, then climbing at the gym, grocery shopping, bicycling between each destination, and a cozy movie and dinner.

And if we never know one another, that will be fine for you have lit up my month, and for that I bow in thanks.

But if I do know you, watch out, for I will light up your already bright life, and we may burn together, like wax paper.

chapter sixteen.

Things I would not yet like to Know about the Future.

"What is going to be is what is,

That is love.

There is no fear of leaping into the immeasurable space of love.

Fall in love?

Or, are you in love?

Such questions cannot be answered

Because in the peace of an all-pervading presence

No one is in and no one is falling in.

No one is possessed by another." ~ Chögyam Trungpa

When it comes to the Future: I would not like our love to be about infatuation or money or time. I will only ask you to marry

~

me if it is right, if our hearts fit together like legos, separable yet complementary.

How long will I love you?

We cannot know. But as the song goes, *longer if I can.*

I would not like to know if it will work out, I would not like to know if we grow old and white-haired and weatherbeaten together. For our love will not be about the romance in movies, it will be about us.

And we will not be about us, but rather we would like to walk a path of service, and a life of gentle smiles in all weathers.

And so I will walk one step at a time, left, right...but not carefully—rather, as if I were entering a wide dance floor and you were on the other end, which you are (if the dance floor is time and space). You are wearing a dress that hugs your body, a simple dark blue dress out of ten dresses that you spent twenty minutes too long choosing. And you chose well. Your hair is cut short in the front, this is new, and I like it, and you do not mind if anyone likes it, which is what makes you so likeable. It is the same with the lilt at the end of your laughter, the wink in your joke, the shrug in your smooth shoulders. You could not care less, and that is what will first draw me to you.

No. What will first draw me to you will be sense-able, sensory, sensual: your hair, or eyes, or laugh, or legs, or the way you lean back in your chair, or our conversation about politics and economy and social justice, or the reason I read in my tub...

…and before we know it the proud old red velvet couch will hold you on one end and me on the other and a dog in the middle and another below and popcorn popped with coconut oil and children's laughter and my booming voice, banning iPhones from the house yet again. And my right hand will fold about your gray socks, your favorite socks that have just been dog-chewed.

> *"I wonder if the snow loves the trees and fields,*
> *that it kisses them so gently? And then it covers them up*
> *snug, you know, with a white quilt; and perhaps it says*
> *'Go to sleep, darlings, till the summer comes again.'"*
> *~ Lewis Carroll*

I would not yet like to know the color of your eyes.

I would not like to know if your skin is dark, or smooth, or if your eyes may be blue, or hazel, or your hair may be yellow, or black, or brown, or short, or long, or curly, or parted in the middle, or fro'd. I would not care to know if you may be tall, or if your nose might be cute, or proud, or you may be short and strong. You may wear duck boots when we go for a little hike through the perfect snow that has quieted our town below and made it look gold-lit, cozy and slow, like a town out of the past.

I would not like to know if things will go well, because things cannot go well, always.

I would like to know that we live each moment with appreciation that each moment is full, yet fragile, golden.

When I am lazy I will not be lazy, for you. When I am weak I will find strength, for you. When I am frustrated I will find the door and walk out of it, for you, and go for a walk and remember the clouds and forget my thoughts and remember my breath and forget your supposed insult and so remember my humor and big-ness and charm and forget my pettiness and my pride and my self-concern. A breath where no breathing was. And I would like to be back in two-and-a-half minutes, for that is how long it takes.

I would not like to know how our sex life is, how many times we do it a week, how many foolishly-named children we have, or whose turn it is to make breakfast (it is mine) or do the dishes (I would prefer to always do them together, I will wash, or rinse and dry and I will sing a song I learned as a child).

So you take the high road...

And I'll take the lowwww rooooad...

And I'll be in Shhcotland afooore yeeee...

Forrr me an' my true love...

will never meet again...

On the bonnie, bonnie bankshh of Loch Lomond.

I would like to know if you notice the breeze that comes through the window, or if you would like to sleep with the curtains open and blinds up or if you like to wear my pajamas (for wearing flannel pajamas two sizes too big is the right size), or if you teach or garden or need to work on the other end of our globe for a year.

Bamboo tilts when the wind blows, it is strong but does not break, it is not rigid, it bows with strength.

I would like you to know that when I work too long, I work for the world, and the world is the inheritance of our children— and our children, whether one or two or three or four or five or more of them, whether popular or bookish, or both…are your first love.

I would like you to know that you are the officer in our home, and I am the sergeant, and they are the troops, and we are an

157.

army of troublemakers in service of good humor and…chaos!

I would not like to know if you have an affair, for if you did, that is a wrong turn, and I am not your love, and the brass locks shall change, for there are second chances at most things, and some plants can survive a cold night out of doors but I am not one of them.

Life is hard and sharp and it hurts, but there are some who wear it lightly, and mindfully, and with class, and are frank yet wise yet light, and if our recipe is right our household shall be one of the hardy and cheerful ones. Life is often lonely and sad and unfair, but if we are lucky we shall work hard and earn our luck, and when we are hit broadside we shall return fire as we sail away with the wind at our backs, and trouble shall find it is bored with us.

Life is long and lineage is longer, and life is short but tradition is weighty but fragile, and we shall care for the things that deserve our care. The look in your eyes when I kiss you on our bed— calm, open—it is a look I shall guard and cultivate, for if I lose it we are lost.

Our sex is not an act—it is a passion that needs itching, and if I lose that itch, I know I had better take better care of our hearth and mantle.

Life will get busy but I am strong—I will be rich and generous and active but quiet sometimes, too. I shall balance making speeches with reading books and drinking coffee with drinking tea and I will play with our children hour after hour and day after day and week after week, they shall distract me from our greatness but I will serve anyway, working in my attic castle with the foldout ladder that drops out of the ceiling.

You will come home one day and find I have cut half a circle in the second floor's floor, and have installed a climbing wall. You will not be so sure.

These words are words, only, but they help me trace the outlines of your as yet unknown face and invisible red heart, like an old-fashioned frilly pressed paper Valentine card.

You are in the high white cold hard mountains, and I am just below, in these Great, Golden Plains—beware: for I am coming for you.

chapter seventeen.

Things I would like to do with You Beneath the Ocean.

"Love creates the unity of heaven and earth.

Love tears apart heaven and earth.

Is love sympathy.

Is love gentleness.

Is love possessiveness.

Is love sexuality.

Is love friendship.

Who knows?"

~ Chögyam Trungpa

I would like to drink tea with you.

It will be late so you will drink something non-caffeinated.

~

You set the kettle on in my kitchen. It will be late so I will drink white tea, just a little caffeine, I am tired, we had dinner in a cozy Tibetan restaurant, I have not slept enough in weeks, and I would like to stay up for you.

It will be our first night, together.

I would like to watch Sherlock with you, as we drink our tea slowly, warming our hands. Or we could watch an old movie: Cary Grant, or Ginger Rogers and Fred Astaire, Toshiro Mifune, or Groucho Marx, or Paul Newman and Robert Redford.

But: *Would it be okay if we cuddled, a little*, you will say.

We drink our tea hurriedly.

It is cold. It is January. We go upstairs. We get in bed. We get warm.

I show you the blankets, one by one, peeling them back, off of you. Four are heavy, from Hudson Bay: two of them are bright red with a black stripe, two are white with yellow, red and green stripes. Another is light and blue and white, knitted for my mother by a hundred-year-old blind lady. I tell you about them, one by one, as I fold them back, off of you.

I love you…a little, I will say less than two weeks later, and it will become a joke between us.

The snow falls from the skies, settling over and into the pine and spruce trees and sidewalks and up against wide curving ancient maples and cottonwoods in white, light sparkles.

~

I pronounce my "t's"—*button, mitten, bitten, written.*

And Red dog will curl up on my bed and help you stay warm and he will sigh and snore softly.

~

This would be our life in my mountain valley town, together, if you were not to live as you do now, away, against the bluegray cold eastern ocean. On weekends we might drive to hot springs, or bus to the Cow City with our bikes and do city things.

~

The blankets are gone. Before we get cold, I would like to move into you and over you, my hand under your red striped white tank top stretched over your breasts, your peaceful sky eyes wide beneath me in the dark. Your dark eyes still and empty, the look of openness. The look of love is a look that cannot be faked. We tumble. Your hair falling over me in the dark, your arching breasts, your bright stomach, our turning, and the feeling between us: we are dancing closely held, moving as if in a waltz, only with much less elegance. Less prescribed.

~

I bow and ask permission, then pick the mountain's sage and crush it between my fingers, cup my hands, smell it with appreciation and put it in my jacket's left breast pocket. Same with the juniper. I thank the high trees.

~

A quiet life, full of parties, and noise, and laughter, and coffee, and conversations in the street, and climbing, and running over the mountain trails with Red dog, and vegan nachos and hoppy beer, or gabby farmers' market lunches on the lawn, and many dark nights lit by community events, or fundraisers, or my working quietly in the attic as I have done for so many years. But when I come down from writing and you come up from your things…I know what comes next: I will kiss your plush lips and your wet tongue and the underside of your top lip and I will lightly bite your ears, breathing hot air into them and you will wriggle and attack me with laughing kisses as I will kiss the underside of your neck and your nipple and then your other and then I will put my hand down upon you, first over your jeans and then later under. I would like to stand and move into you against doorframes in the kitchen and on the floor in back dark room and the entrance and on the balcony outside you will say *people will see* but I am protective and they will not. My hands against your back pulling at your clothes, my hands in your thick dark hair and you will say, *I like how you touch me*, and I know you do, for it is that dance, separately and together.

A dance of passion—words sound so easily cliché but I would like to mean what I say. And so I mean the words that I say to you: it *is* a dance, and it is a dance that builds a movement of passion, if passion is water, heated by fire. Fire until you are wet and I am overripe and your hands are full with mine.

But sex is a small part of a relationship: and a relationship is a small, but significant part of a life well-lived.

The main thrust of our lives together shall be to walk a rocky path, barefoot, together. I would like the woman who I am to ask to join me on this mountain journey to be brave, patient, sharp. A caring human. I would like you to help me and I would like to be able to help you to be of service. I would not like to commit to a love affair that distracts either of us from helping this poor, endlessly confused, ungrateful, self-righteous, critical, speedily shallow yet fundamentally good world. In this, our world, we are all skimming the surface of the life each of us could live. We are lonely, but many of us, we are not friends with this, our loneliness. Not yet. We skim along our precious life instead of swimming down into the sadjoy ocean…beneath the movement of the heavy ocean. I would like for us to discover our basic goodness, instead of nervously searching for an itch to scratch or clinging to a momentary hit of external happiness while we push away pain. When reality is right here: your soft, beautiful, decent raw red heart.

And that is what I would like to offer you, if you are brave—I shall serve as a mirror for you, because I care for you. I would like to let you finally see what has been hidden from your searchingly hungry gaze: your red heart.

And if that is what you would like to offer me, then this is why my red heart will break open beneath your flooded ocean.

This precious life circles in ceaseless interdependence and impermanence: we cannot claim solidity, but I can commit to swimming, with you, beneath the waves.

~

Close your eyes.

> "…*Maybe the rock knows,*
>
> *Sitting diligently on earth,*
>
> *Not flinching from cold snowstorms or baking heat.*
>
> *O rock,*
>
> *How much I love you:*
>
> *You are the only loveable one.*
>
> *Would you let me grow a little flower of love on you?"*
>
> ~ *Chögyam Trungpa*

Things I would like to do with You on a Snowy Weekend.

"What good is the warmth of summer without the cold of winter to give it sweetness?" ~ John Steinbeck

Friday night begins when the night ends: with you.

The snow still falls from the skies in white, light sparkles, settling against the trees and sidewalks and up against the wide curving ancient trees. The falling snow shows off as it slowly cameos through dark yellow triangles beneath each street light, bringing with it quiet magic.

It is night: I would like to   you. I would like to bounce and tickle and laugh and bite and be bitten and squeeze and marinate in you.

It is Saturday morning: when we wake I would like to help you button up the front of your prim dress, cotton, starched. You tie your hair in an elegant whirlwind, or pull it straight to the side.

You are simple, and simple is love.

What is love? I do not know. I would like to know. And how we find out is by living our day fully, again and again.

Whether together or apart it does not matter.

When we wobble downstairs you will shiver, and turn on the heat and make coffee and I will put on big boots over my long johns and a big hat over my vertical hair and Red dog and I will go out into the white. And I would like to shovel the walk with the yellow metal snowshovel while Red dog pees happily, trotting about. Snow always makes him happy.

It is still snowing. I would like to come in and drink water and lemon, and coffee with you and meditate and we get our swimsuits on and tip toe outside through the snow and jump in the hot tub and read new *New Yorkers*. Now we eat too much hot, sweet-smelling cinnamon raisin bread. It is Saturday so we message our friends and we bike to meet them at a snowed-in golden café, where we will see unplanned friends, too.

I would like to eat with you, talk with you, laugh with you, debate with you. I would like to admire your style and your

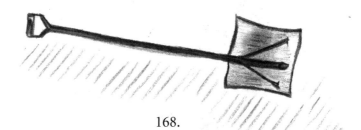

elegant arching eyebrow and inelegant laugh as you sit before a red brick wall with a white and black clock with a red arrowed second hand circling behind you.

I would like to be apart from you and do my things, and I would like you to be separate from me—as oxygen is to fire, space is to our delight for one another.

I would like to visit you in the big old black n'white Gray Skyscraper City on Valentine's and I would like to see you in your town at your favorite café. I would like to drink more coffee born one continent off, but roasted only thirty feet away in a handsome century-old roaster.

If you let me, I would like to have five children with you, though I would settle for three.

If I let you, you may hold my heart in your hands. It is messy, but beautifully red. Please do not drop it.

I would like it to work, or not to work—if it works, that is love. If it runs out, it is not. For love is not a thing, it is not merely the present moment—love is a string of a thousand, thousand present moments—an un-ending string of Christmas lights, powered by the Sun itself.

If our love runs out, you shall find another. If our love runs out, I would like to love again.

There is love and there is love, so perhaps love is not the question. Perhaps the question is time.

chapter nineteen.

Things I would like to do with You on Valentine's Day.

"True love is eternal, infinite, and always like itself. It is equal and pure, without violent demonstrations: it is seen with white hairs and is always young in the heart." ~ Honoré de Balzac

I would like to celebrate forty or fifty more Valentine's Days, with you.

But I have not met you, yet.

I would like to meet you in the Old Harbor, or the Far-off Ocean Harbor, or in the Gray Skyscraper City, or in High Lake Lands, or in Fog City, or in All Light or All Dark City, or in Café City, or in Empire City or northern Tweed, or on a sailboat off the west coast of Mountain Peninsula, or on the top of a low continent, or in my mountain valley, or in any place that I have been or have not yet ever been.

~

I would like to see you in my home, or in your apartment, and in our future home together. I would like to buy you a potted plant instead of a plastic-wrapped dozen roses shipped and flown from far away where they were sprayed with poisons by mask-less underpaid laborers—I would like our romance to be as healthy in its roots as it is beautiful on the surface.

I would like to make love to you without touching you (much, for most of the day). From the first words and kiss and breath in the yellow sunshine morning to the shower and dogwalk and commuting (bicycle) to work, to dinner and a cozy movie or music, I would like to flirt and charm and cuddle, and entice and be enticed.

It is February and the snow is cold and the sun is gold and the afternoon roads are dirt slush—Winter is undecided, thinking it may become Spring, already.

As you know I would like for you to be tall, and pale but with red cheeks when you've exercised or come in from the cold or I would like for you to be cherrydark, and smooth, or with long rich hair or curly dark hair or straight hair—your eyes are green, and light, or dark amber—the color of bourbon sipping at home on our loveseat reading too-long-ignored books, or whatever we drink too much of, too quickly, while playing happy hour free pool in the basement bar. I would not like to care what you look like, I would like to care how you look into me.

I would like to unbutton your oxford blue shirt dress and I would like to bend you down and up and I would like you to

arch your back and make sounds in a strangely formal, sweet way, and when I bite your ear, lightly, or breathe into it, you shiver from down south straight up into your heaven. And I would like to take your dress back and expose your heart and, later, I would like to find a soft tee shirt for you to sleep in. Every night before we sleep I would like to look at the white moon or clouds or branches against the quiet night and feel the fresh breeze upon my cooled shoulders. Before I turn to sleep, I would like to sit up and meditate and dedicate another day.

I would like many things! I would like to love you, this Valentine's. But you are too far away and you are too new to me and too unknown to me.

⁓

"Keep love in your heart. A life without it is like a sunless garden when the flowers are dead. The consciousness of loving and being loved brings a warmth and richness to life that nothing else can bring." ~ Oscar Wilde

Perhaps you live, work or play close by, but I do not yet know your story, your family, your books on your bookshelf, your photographs, your habits and what you like to make for breakfast. I like rhubarb oatmeal.

Or perhaps you do not exist, and I shall be an old man wearing a strange hat and smoothed denim rocking in a chair (it will help my old back), staring out at my vague memories of my handsome uneven lucky busy exhausting funny youth. An old man, I look out with foolish eyes at my faded hope and sunsets gone dark, and so finally.

Now, I am at a time when I would like children. First I would like to get to know you: I would like to travel for months at a go with you. I would like to enjoy ups and downs with you and know that we know how to sail, together, in all weathers.

I am at a time when I care for Red dog—my best friend—more than all but two dozen human friends. For our fellow humans we hold to high standards. Humans forgive and are forgiven less easily than we forgive wayward rascally dogs.

I work long and late and often…I feel this day seeping away,

I feel this life pouring through my tired hands like water—I cannot hold it back. But I *can* drink the water: it is cool and refreshing to drink you in, to stare into your ocean eyes, to glance at the dusty postcards of women who no longer love me as I take them off of my orange refrigerator and put them away in a shoebox.

I am ready for love, but not yet marriage. I am ready for friendship, but not yet love. I am ready for romance, but not yet for arguments and making up and patience and jealousy and compromises…

…I wonder if when I kiss you how I will know if we will get to kiss one another forty years from now. I am ready.

I am confident at this cliff, and I dive into space, out of my cozy life. I dive to you and fly.

And so, this Valentine's Day, the best laid plans unmade, I bow before the February snow, your youth and our confidence…this Valentine's Day, I say *I love you*, whoever you are.

All that lies between you and I is time, and time is a mist, and it is morning, and it is late Winter, and the day and the season shall warm, and I would like to see you soon.

> *"You don't love someone for their looks, or their clothes, or for their fancy car, but because they sing a song only you can hear." ~ not Oscar Wilde*

175.

Things I would like to do
with You Indoors.

*"Of course I'll hurt you. Of course you'll hurt me.
Of course we will hurt each other. But this is the very
condition of existence. To become spring, means
accepting the risk of winter. To become presence,
means accepting the risk of absence."*
~ Antoine de Saint-Exupéry

Outside it is gathering fog that is not fog but blizzard—I saw it coming while I was bicycling home through the fading light, the storm flowing down the mountain canyon.

We can turn off my home's heat: we will need to sweat together to keep one another warm.

You can bake, with cinnamon and brown sugar or molasses or maple syrup, and I will help break up the pecans. But I will eat most of what I break so you kick me out but I do not leave,

I interfere with your apron.

I would like to touch your mouth, and then listen to it.

It is full, and pink, or is it red? Or is it slightly purple, or orange? I cannot tell—your make up is subtle. Your eyebrows are not— they are dark and fine, yet bold.

Words, words: these are merely pretty words. Your eyebrows are garish, yet musical. How is that?

Your hair is long, and wild, and messy (I like it that way). You are good at this, and that, and this, and that: you are your own muse.

> *February: the holiday lights have all gone dark. No presents. No family, no cheer. But the cold makes us stronger, and more appreciative when the hot days and candy-colored flowers do return. This is not the time to escape to a postcard beach blue ocean island vacation.*

> *This is a time to feel your hunger. A time to finally focus in on what you dream of. Forget entertainment. Fun can be a distraction—there will be time for lounging with umbrella drinks and finally learning to surf. When I will pick you up after I scuba dive for the first time, you whisper: let's go home…and I agree. But not now.*

> *Now is your time for getting it done.*

I would like to look into your quiet eyes, or are they full, the daylight would tell me but it is dark, and I am lying next to you, listening to you rant about something I do not care about.

~

Perhaps you are neurotic: you are wild, you are careless in the way that beautiful children who grow up in safe neighborhoods are. As a child, in Winter you slid on your sled down the middle of your street, unafraid of traffic. Or in Summer you played Horse on a hoop set safely in front of your house, ball on hip and moody smile when a car dared drive down your exclusive street.

> *February here is all too dead and gray, and Winter now*
> *is too long and cold. Snow upon snow. But that is what*
> *Winter is. Patience is not patient until it has been too long.*
> *Hold on to your wool blanket, dress warmly. Now is your*
> *season to focus: even Winter is getting tired, though it*
> *appears indefatigable.*

I would make love into you, but I must be careful—you light me up like dry paper, and I dare not get too close. But, like paper, too, I dare not pause once I am too close, or I shall burn up without even touching your flame with my tongue. I am hungry for you. It is late and I am full and I should not eat you, but I want to, and you want to, so we enjoy a second helping.

You must sometimes go far away: space is all that protects you from me.

You are unfairly talented: the gods put all their powers into your red clay, leaving a thousand others beige. But I am an arrogant mortal (was it Prometheus?) who would like to challenge the high gods, and we shall marry and birth a little half-god, a demi-god, and even as you burn me up I smile into your fiery eyes.

179.

chapter twenty.

I have been tested and beaten but still I come back. I have walked a long time, and alone, but still I keep walking. I have never given up or even come close to giving up, really: even when I have come close to giving up, my core was warm.

Your style is top of the low continent, 1920s; or Café City with long cigarettes and languid talk of intellectual revolution, or 1970s' Second Wave feminism with too-large glasses and narrow slacks with wide bottoms, tall boots, or a dress and a leather purse and a silk blouse. Your style is black and white, but you paint in color.

We like to swim: I wriggle and pull and gain strength under the water. I know why you are a mermaid, and I would like to fish you, but I like fish, so I do not fish you.

You have questionable taste in boys, which means I stand a chance. My smile is wide and crooked with you, and my voice grows loud and my throat hurts—life is a bruising affair and I grin my way through the line.

Bicycling through salt, slush, over ice and packed snow, gray snow, tan snow, black snow, snow. Dismounting when there is too much snow, and walking virginal prints into the quiet white night snowfall, yellow streetlights and your warm beating heart far away in your second-floor apartment: I can still hear it but only when you listen for mine.

Your neck is kissable, it is a better thing to kiss than your dark lips, because I like to hear you talk.

I would make love to your mind, and argue with it, and when we are tired and sweaty, salt, sweat, water, we would dive one, two, splash, ripple, into the pale turquoise saltwater ocean.

I climb, when I have a spare hour. I bicycle between things. I sail from shore to shore. I work too hard for too long, and smoke rises from my bent but fit body. I go to yoga and unbend and open. But at the end of eleven years I still see another mountain above, and I am tired. I am patient, and walk like an elephant, with slow modesty and exertion, but I would bend into you, instead of my cool sheets, I would bend into your breasts and sigh into your chest, if you were asleep, and I would take you out and charm you, and take you in and we would play. And we would pray into our orgasm, instead of into myth, our heaven is right here, it is not found in postcard vacations or above vacant clouds circling a mountain peak or, even, in books that smell of coriander.

I would steal poetry from your heart, and leave it for you to read with tea, your heart, my words, bound in a book of tan paper.

I would make love into you in the morning, and in the evening, and if you wake, we would make love, and if I awake, I will pull you to me.

I would like you sharp, and I would like you soft. I would like you to challenge me, even as you enjoy me. I would like you sweet. I would like to hear your laughter: laughter of fire plus space, space enough for two to fly together, instead of crowding our wings into one another's path.

My words have all been offered, as a prayer, once, twice, eleven times, a thousand times: but they are my mantra, and you are my practice, and our cherry love may be our fruition.

Or, it may not.

Either way, Spring will rise.

But not yet.

"Hello darkness, my old friend

I've come to talk with you again…"

~ Simon & Garfunkel

chapter twenty-one.

Things I would like to Read at the End of my List.

"Two things are needed to achieve great things: a plan, and not quite enough time." ~ Leonard Bernstein

This is where I am at. I must be close to the end of my list of loves.

I would like to get through this list and see your name, finally.

Once I meet you, whoever you are, the list is ended.

I am nervous and shy around you. I am confident and charming around you.

I would like to kiss you first just tentatively, tentatively, your confidence makes me excitedly careful, subdued…I reach for my humor but it is napping. And so I stand and gently and heavily press my feet upon our Earth, and She will guide me into your laughter and through our conversation. You agree to let me take you out: we go to the new eco restaurant that I like

~

because it marks "V" and has big portions and good coffee and endless hot sauce.

Dinner is good and goes quickly. You drink saké and I drink saké and you drink more saké and I drink much more saké and then, dessert.

Dessert is the time for us to decide if, later, soon, we would like to undress one another.

Outside through the windows we see golden lights. The windygray evening—fast!—turns to black, wet night.

I pretend to walk you home while you pretend to want to go home: instead we walk to my home.

Along the way I show you the old wide gray tree that I like: you cannot even see the top, it is so tall! It would have been young more than a hundred years ago, when men in top hats and women in ridiculous dresses and horses and carriages passed by its then-thin gray trunk and green leaves.

We stand close together, so close we see only eyes. You lean against gray bark. Above us: the tree's naive first buds. It is March and it will snow again and they will suffer for their exuberance!

I would like to kiss your strong neck: it is regal, like a Morgan horse. I would like to hold your hands, and lift our arms above and against the tree. We kiss again.

I would like to hold your head as we kiss for the first time and soon the fiftieth time beneath the old gray tree.

But it is too sweet too quick and so, soon, we pretend we would just like to talk, and walk. We talk along the creek, and walk more as the damp darkness tries to make you shiver. We have dressed for one another instead of dressing for the wet weather.

I would like to study your eyes: they hold mysteries and lamps in them.

If you are She, then you are the last name on the List of Loves that I will read, in this life.

We all have a list of names of those we have dated. So I ask her out, and her, and her, and we go out, or we hike, or we whatever: and it is a great first date, or an okay one, or a weak one, or a false one; and so we go out again or we do not. And the List lengthens or shortens as life ripples backward or forward, a receding or advancing tide.

I must be close to the end of my List: I am running my fingers over the thin end of this scroll. And this joyous, heartbreaking, or ordinary list of affairs must soon conclude with one name.

Yours.

What is your name?

> *"We're all a little weird. And life's a little weird. And when we find someone whose weirdness is compatible with ours, we join up with them and fall into mutually-satisfying weirdness—and call it love—true love."*
> *~ Robert Fulghum*

When I meet you and you meet me I do not know if you are the last name on the List of Loves, or if you are to be nobody to me, or if you are to be just another name on this long List.

I do not think that I have met you, yet. Where will I meet you? When? Will it be because I decide to go right instead of left one day, and get some groceries, or go left instead of right, to dinner or drinks or a café or a party instead of home?

Love hangs on the intertwined threads of limitless mutual coincidences: love is not a good business plan.

When you are the last name on the List your name will be held close, and the List will be tossed: it will serve as kindling in our fireplace in our hearth.

You and I have not yet realized that we are the two human beings who will enjoy saying nothing together, being apart from one another together, having too many breakfasts together, drinking one too many drinks together, going horseback riding together, doing laundry together, doing parties together, raising children together, composting neurosis for awake together.

We do not either of us know who our best friend in this world in this life will be…yet: it is me and it is you.

Your mahogany cerulean or light-brown or sea-green eyes are really somewhere, right now.

The other night the moon looked at your face and you waited in the open air for me to move at you—I did not. The other night I took you up against the back of the couch and we laughed, after. After love your hair is messy, long, curling gently; it used to be braided but now it is a baroque disaster.

The other names on the List were a lifetime ago, so many lifetimes, so many dates and beds and moonlit conversations, you in a robe opening, you in the fields above a cliff above Old Harbor City, you in a shop in the land of Green Mountains, you half naked in a stream, you in the pouring rain against the black iron fence, you bending, rocking, giggling, opening, opening, opening…so many good and heartbreaking days and nights in the names on this sweetsadlonghardcynicalgood scroll.

I would like to take my time, though I cannot wait.

Last night, alone, with you out there, I watched a movie, beneath blankets with Red dog sleeping below. The heroine reminded me of you who I have not yet met. She was strong and soft. *Human* is more attractive than perfect, because it is real.

And she reminded me that the end of this List can be shortened by keeping those off of it who I am not in line with, ethically. My bar ought to be set high—not merely for attraction, but for attraction and friendship, both.

And so I do not care for the color of your hair or any of it! It is no matter. I will look for what you care for. What does matter is what you want to do with who you are. And, of course, if you care for me.

I will treasure your hair, and your eyes, and your little nose, and your mouth, and the back of your neck, and your strong legs, and your eyebrows: it is fun. But I would like you to know that what is important is what is important and we can laugh at the rest so we can enjoy our row in the boat across the stream.

The alchemy that is friendship mixed with attraction is important. The alchemy that is two hearts, two minds, two lives, two particular laughs in silly melody is important.

And, it is yet unknown—as you are, to me.

"One day I will find the right words, and they will be simple." ~ Jack Kerouac

chapter twenty-two.

Things I would like to do with You this Springtime.

"When spring came, even the false spring, there were no problems except where to be happiest.

The only thing that could spoil a day was people and if you could keep from making engagements, each day had no limits.

People were always the limiters of happiness, except for the very few that were as good as spring itself."
~ Ernest Hemingway

This is Spring: it is cold, it is warm, it is gray above. Now it is sunny. At night, I hear the rain.

Yesterday, the flowers were blooming. The day before that, it snowed again—for the last time, I think. Suddenly, today, the stark thin deadlike branches have budded: sticky bright green. Each morning, the birds' song wakes me and the sun blinds

189.

my bed's old white wool blankets…but the cool breeze lets me dream one more dream.

And I am tired. And this is Spring.

I would like to look at your eyes, not into them—I am still sleepy, shy beneath the hot morning sun of our new love. Only a week ago, I swam the swamp of Alone. Only a week ago I would wake cold, thinking of a love I did not have. Sure: during the day I saw friends and laughed and joked and listened, but then again I was alone as soon as my friends returned to their lives. I shopped for and ate dinner alone. I went to bed alone. I woke with loneliness.

But then I met you, a fresh yet familiar sight as you approached me and my beautiful friend in the square.

This morning is only one week later and yet living my life is like reading a different book. This morning, waking to your hands praying before your closed eyes, I am foolish with giddy gratitude. Your eyes are the green seen through the blue ocean water on a vacation I have not yet taken; or they are the grayblack of the moon's shadow on a warm Spring evening.

It is bright in my morning bedroom and I am scared of losing you to reality, so I take the sheet over our heads for another moment of naked dreams together. Your body in the shade is varnished sailboat wood. I rest my hand on the side of your thigh and say, "Good morning." You touch my face with seafoam nails and say nothing. In the bright shade, your dark red lips do not smile.

You just look and I am pleasantly surprised.

I have seen this look twice or three times before: you look *in love.*

> **"On soft Spring nights I'll stand in the yard under the stars**
>
> **Something good will come out of all things yet**
>
> **And it will be golden and eternal just like that**
>
> **There's no need to say another word." ~ Jack Kerouac**

Later, our love would roll and fall and shatter and float and rise and finally tangle, for years off and on. And though it rose high, it ended as low as all our little loves.

I have lost so many sweet hearts because of miscommunication, because of my focus on work, because of distance, because of one drink too many, because of an awkward fear, or simply because a good relationship has run its course.

And yet like a wintry wolf, I can smell the Spring. And I still feel She is out there. A complement, a fun friend to dance with.

I do not look for perfection: She is not on the map. I do look for dry wood, coupled with fire (friendship, and lust) gathered together in a hearth (a common vision of being of benefit to others) coupled with, someday, a good armchair and a hot drink

⌒

(family). All I require is one match to kindle it.

But do not rush: I have my work, my home, my life—and I love the living of it.

I do not write these words to sound sicklysweet, emotional, or even romantic. I write truth and whatever comes out comes out and I am this.

I would like to know you, but you are not here. You are on the map, but I do not know where to search. I am where the Great golden, now-suburb-filled Plains join the High Red Mountains, in this green valley full of Victorians.

It has been a lifetime since I have seen you.

You will return.

> *"Do I let her sleep or should I wake her up?*
> *You said: We both go together if one falls down.*
> *Yeah, right…I talk out loud like you're still around.*
> *Oh, no, no…and I miss you."*
> *~ West Coast, Coconut Records.*

Spring is the coming together of Winter and Summer—it is the powerful pause then sudden snap and unfurling, the wholesome pain of birth, the delighted cycle of youth, a been-too-long sunshine day followed by wet snow over humbled flowers.

I would like to meet you at a party. An art party. You are in a room with a friend of mine and another friend of yours. I walk in, make a joke, we start talking, I start trying to talk your language, because you are not from here. I am clumsy at it, but better than one would think. You are flattering, tall, stylish, foreign, new: a Spring flower. I have recently been dropped for not communicating, not being available, and I understand and I am happy with my freedom, but sad at losing my life and my heart to my work again, again.

Too few flowers value a plot of land worked over by old tools and oxen and heavy boots to make food for others.

The party is large and bright and self-consciously hip, which is insecure and pretentious but…I am a warrior, and I recognize subtle aggression (*poverty mentality*) when I see it. I know many, here—I am charming, relaxed, loud and I look for you again, after our first conversation. But you are surrounded by your friends, my friends, and there is no full moment to flirt further. And so I go to another party, and another bar, and I forget you.

But I wake up in the sunshine, in my gray sheets, and I remember you. But I do not know how to contact you, and so I forget you.

But the memory of your eyes blinds my forgetfulness, and I remember you.

But you are gone.

And then, two days later, in the midst of a big busy day, I bicycle downtown: late for a late lunch meeting. I talk with friends on the way in, and sit down for my meeting. And then, talking to

~

the restaurant's manager, I see you. You are sitting in the corner with three friends, one of them little.

This is a little magic: because you are gone to me, and do not live here. But you are here.

You get up and I talk with you, your bright eyes nearly blinding my eyes. We smile and say things. I make funny faces and play with and hide from and search for the little girl who is at your table. I politely say *hello* to the older lady, and to your younger friend. Sometimes I am not charming, but today I am charming. And, mostly, I talk with you. When we talk we are on our own, and the world blurs. I try and mostly fail to speak your language, and you enjoy my trying and mostly failing. We are mutually amused.

I return to my meeting. Later, finished, you begin to leave the restaurant, and though my meeting continues, I turn as you pass and say, "You can't leave without saying 'bye, that'd be rude," smiling into you. You smile back: "I didn't want to be rude, you were in a meeting." I say, "Well, then, you're rude either way." I stand up and straight up ask for your number, and you put it into my phone. You are leaving tomorrow morning for the far-away Gray Skyscraper City.

But you are returning in a month.

In the meantime we first text and then write long letters and get to know.

How little we all know one another.

~

And you ask things about me, and I tell you about myself. I do not know why I tell you so much truth, but you are beautiful and I am tired—though I am attached, too, to my alone-ness. The longing is here: the longing for a match, for a friend, for a gold lover to stretch out on my gray sheets. The longing to love and even bicker about the little things: the longing is right here.

"I've been waiting on you...

As it breaks, the summer will wake

But the Winter washed what's left of the taste

As it breaks, the summer will warm

But the Winter craved what's lost

Crave what's all...gone Away." ~ Future Islands

Summertime will come: the heat will inspire us to wear very little and swim. I will be as-if tan, my freckles will just about all join as-if into one. Still, I will mostly work in too-cold overly air-conditioned cafés (swamp coolers and passive solar shade and breezes are far preferable).

And I will love some of you with some of me, and then all of you with all of me, if you let me and if I let you, as we get to know.

And I hope we each have the honor, and pleasure to feel sad, and joy, and lust, together...and lunch on the green lawn beneath the big trees by the white creek at the farmers' market, together. I like dumplings with too much hot sauce.

There is nothing sweeter than warm sadness, than waking on a Saturday morning to rumpled sheets and an agenda for two.

"I got that summertime, summertime sadness."
~ Lana del Rey

chapter twenty-three.

Things I would like to Sing with You.

"Am I in love? No. I thought I been in love but I guess I wasn't; it just passed over. I guess I haven't met the girl yet, but I will—and I hope I won't be too long 'cause I get lonesome sometimes. I get lonesome right in the middle of a crowd. And I got a feeling that, that with her—whoever she may be—I won't be lonesome no matter where I am."
~ Elvis Presley, 1956, just before stardom hit.

I would like to remember that I do not look for love to fill a hole: that is for new bitter mint that I plant in my home's rain-nurtured dirt this still-sunny, early Spring evening.

No: we cannot look for a lover to make happiness that we do not already know.

Rather I would like to learn that love is about partnership. Love does not displace space. Love is not a crutch.

197.

⌒

You will not complete me; nobody can.

But.

Love is a dance! Space, flirtation, tenderness. An elegant actress leaning softly, tired, into a reserved gentleman on a silver screen. And at the end of the flick her regal eyes meet his eyes—wet, still, staring for so long.

So, yes.

I would like to learn if you like beachsand—the feel of it. I would like to know the strength or smoothness of your hands because I hold them with full appreciation of your gift to me of who you are. You have chosen to spend some of your life with me. I would like to listen for and trust in your small judgments, and I would like to miss you like the wet breeze before the rain when you are away, which may be often.

I would like to share some of the many things I am passionate about just with you...and feel you feel the joy I feel in these favorite things.

I would like to find respite in our match: for you and I will both be busy, and full of vigor in service, sailing tireless seas all our little long lives...

...but, so.

I must first learn to love you, which would require you to tame me, and which would require that I swim the heavy ocean beneath your young waves.

Things I would like to Sing with You.

~

"This bitter earth—

Well, what a fruit it bears.

Ooooooh…

And if my life is like the dust

Ooh that hides the glow of a rose

What good am I?

Heaven only knows

No, this bitter Earth

Yes, can be so cold

Today you're young

Too soon—you're old

But while a voice

Within me cries

I'm sure someone

may answer my call

And this bitter earth ooooooh

May not be ohhhh, so bitter after all."

~ Dinah Washington

But: you are cautious and I am briefly tired and our moment passes through my fingers like water.

~

Our paths, so briefly braided, seem now to trend left, and bend right and away.

I am thirsty but cannot drink this salt water.

> *"My friend is one who takes me for what I am."*
> *~ Henry David Thoreau*

I met you and you played games (or perhaps you did not) but in any case, though you were close by, you were far away.

I felt my easy charm fall momentarily into tiredness—a kind of tenderness. I would have liked to have rested my head in your lap while you idly played with my hair.

Reg dog circles and circles, curling into a cozy ball, ready for sleep.

Oh how I wanted nothing more than to curl up into a cozy circle within you.

I would like to climb my own hills, jump down my own valleys until I may fully appreciate myself…even when I become tired and boring…when my fast fire is momentarily spent.

But I could not yet be tired, with you: it was too soon, and that was my first mistake. When one plays a game against a poolshark, one's first mistake is one's last mistake—the table is run.

~

"I said, rock, what's a matter with you rock?
Don't you see I need you, rock?"
~ Nina Simone, Sinnerman.

Suddenly I was alone, again, though I had not yet admitted it to myself. Alone again with my work and Red dog and fickle friends, alone again with that tiredness. I would like to cry, bitterly, not sweet like the creamed yellow local honey that I buy from the white-haired jocular joker at the market.

The world cries for heroines—I cry for a single match.

"Let the seasons begin; take the big king down." ~ Beirut

Boys and girls play games with hearts and words.

And silence.

Gentlemen and ladies, however, do not play games. I want to see you, or I do not want to see you? You do not need to play me: you need to just be you and I care for this you.

I would like to listen: to get to know your stories, your life, your dreams, your daily humors small and large—I would like to read your story until like a well-read book your story is well-known to me, the favorite parts wrinkled from the bath or the rain, and dried by the eastern sun.

I would like to laugh with you to joke at you to whisper to you to share with you to walk with you to run with you to climb

~

with you to bicycle with you. To make love with you to dine with you to drink your wine to bathe with you and read with you in the hotel bath.

I would like to kiss you as I see your eyes look into mine.

But they do not. Perhaps we will try again, perhaps not. You are cautious, perhaps because boys have too long too easily fallen in something like love at you.

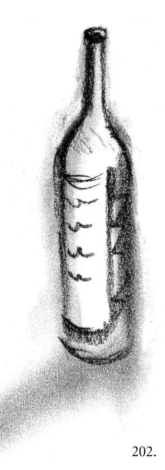

I am a gentleman.

And so though I fall in love I am weathered enough to understand that charm does not win love—it wins laughter and dancing and singing and love-making. But none of this is love, as I explained in your dream.

I know what love is and it is friendship set afire: kindled until it warms us both.

> *"Love is not affectionate feeling, but a steady wish for the loved person's ultimate good as far as it can be obtained." ~ C.S. Lewis*

Love is easy. Love is chemistry—a laboratory. Love is as simple as connecting this together with that. Her brilliant eyes and my heated heart.

But this is not love.

Not yet.

Genuine love resides only in the present moment. Genuine love is everyday.

Genuine love feels no need to entertain the space away.

Genuine love is up, genuine love is down and yet genuine love never wavers.

Love is something else entire. It is caring. It is arguing with curiosity—it is giving an inch when the other seems certainly wrong—it is teasing, it is empathy, it is respect, it is a moment of quiet smiling admiration each morning.

"Funny how a lonely day can make a person say,
'What good is my life?'"
~ Shirley Bassey

I would like to see you one last time. And then again for another hundred times, or two times, or three times, or whatever the math is on countless times.

I would like to play, but not play games. I do not play games because I cannot—they twist my sweet heart like a wet rag, and what feels all right, fast becomes unworthy of us.

I admire you for your as yet unknown talent. For now, that is all: you are a sandcastle, your tide has washed you away, I cannot tell what you were, and so I would like to go swimming hard joyfully up into the salt waves, laughing and relaxed. And though you have left the beach behind you cannot swim with me.

I would like to know you, but the game is lost.

"Underneath a silver moon

With the windows open wide

I can hear the stars go by

And all the while I'm dreaming of

The ballad for my one true love

Searching for the perfect way to say

I love you…"

~ Mason Jennings

Things I would like to See when You Open to Me.

"'Well,' said Pooh, 'what I like best—' and then he had
to stop and think. Because although Eating Honey was
a very good thing to do, there was a moment just
before you began to eat it which was better than when
you were, but he didn't know what it was called."
~ A.A. Milne, Winnie-the-Pooh.

I would like to see you come to my tall old house on the hill. It is the close of a long day and the sky is bright dark blue black, you know. The moon is animated, half hidden behind the clouds.

"The moon will not use the door, only the window."
~ Rumi

You call and I answer, and you visit my house on the hill. We have not seen each other for weeks. But you do not make excuses. And I do not pretend I do not know why you are here. Still, you are tentative. I give you a tour, that ends in my bedroom. You smell like sweat before we start, and I smell like saltwater after we finish.

"Rivers know this: there is no hurry. We shall get there some day." ~ A.A. Milne, Pooh's Little Instruction Book.

Now you are far away. I do not know you. But you are familiar to me. And I am familiar to you.

Love is not now our obstacle. Passion we hold hot together. Timing, however, is in our way.

I would like to rent a car and take Red dog, and take the top down and let all of the sun and wind in—the wind too loud for music—and roadtrip to meet you.

You are too desirable not to be dating another, now, and you deserve the best. I am always dating, but I am always waiting. There is a long line of women with erect posture, with tall legs.

And so when I date, and am inevitably dumped (when she realizes how much I work), or am toyed with by une femme who plays games...I do not long mourn the loss of half of something. I wait for a full something: a *match*.

Match: we will be equal, but our balance will spark fire— humor, passion, insight—from off of one another's hearts.

You are barefoot. I am a prince.

My heart asks yours if it is matched: we have sensed in one another the opening that I have felt before, the opening that people call *love*, but that I call you and me.

"This morning, with her, having coffee." ~ Johnny Cash, when asked for his description of paradise.

I would like to see you in a cabin for ten days.

I would like to rest into your chest. There are a thousand beautiful women and you are one of them but your intellect, your ethics, your easy kindness may raise you to a mountain wreathed by soft clouds where I may fall with you.

I would like to walk in the clouds with you. I would like to be silent with you as we walk the dark forest path beneath the bright sky. I would like to chop wood and carry water. I would like to hang up our wash on a line of twine. I would like for you to make me black coffee that is good. I would like for you to stay in your denim shirt, and nothing much else, all morning. You are okay with that.

Fall in love with her body, it is too hot for sheets, chart her terrain inch by inch—but fall in love with her face, and forget the map.

209.

"I don't want no better book than what your face is."
~ Mark Twain, The Adventures of Huckleberry Finn.

You said: *the first time I saw the forest I cried*. Bears, islands, whales in the water, and trees with the width of the wingspan of three of me. I cannot cry, because I have not yet seen the forest. Show it to me?

And *our* morning agenda will be different than *my* loud mornings back home: here in this cabin, our wooden castle, we will begin the day with kisses before even opening our eyes. If we make coffee first, it will be cold when I am finished with you and you are finished. Then we will swim to get clean. Though I have never skinny dipped I like wearing very little. I like the water: it lets me fly, in slow motion. I jump and I dive and it is too cold and that is just right. You are too skinny, some say, and I am too bitter, the battle has been long...we are just right for one another.

A light kiss of two iridescent butterflies.

I would like to take refuge in these woods. I would like to create a small world that is populated only by two.

And this is how we will begin. It will not all be sex and cooking and aimless wandering through the forest and conversations and happy runs and lazy hours with Red dog and paperback books and pens by the creek...but it will be mostly that.

My heart has no insulation, now—it is open to the weather.

~

When the weather reaches my heart a whisper sounds like a roar, a breeze feels like a storm, an echo tells me of suffering half a world away.

It is all so sad, looking back at the lovers in our lives: the joy, the squabbles, the moments—swimming in the sun so bright the water is clear, laughing sex against the door. They are gone!

It is sweet: smelling lilacs in the Spring. It is delightful meeting one whom I have known in past lives. I do not believe in reincarnation but I do know you already: for our conversation follows the harmonies of old friends.

"And only the enlightened can recall their former lives;
for the rest of us, the memories of past existences are
but glints of light, twinges of longing, passing shadows,
disturbingly familiar, that are gone before they
can be grasped, like the passage of that silver bird..."
~ Peter Matthiessen

Come visit my town and we will play volleyball with new friends, families and children and dogs by the busy creek below a wide, green lawn beneath wide, old cottonwood trees. A mile above our day is nothing but open sky and a big bird, circling silently on an invisible current.

I will take friendship plus attraction any day over falling in love. For I am no fool for fickle: I search for a love that is built of friendship and can withstand the most merciless rains and flooding.

And I will take it all and give it back into you and you will take it all and give it back to me, every day. And if I am given nothing I will give it back: for loneliness is a broken-hearted love affair with *my* life.

I will massage your shoulders with my strong hands that shake, slightly, from too much fresh coffee from this rich earth carrying so much suffering. I grew up trying to massage my uncle's and my father's strong shoulders and my hands grew capable.

My hands relax into your back and neck, and your back and neck relax in my hands. Your hair is long and dark in the shadows of this, our first evening together. Later, your intimacy is dark as you open, to me, but when I turn you over again and breathe into your ear and bite you, light, I see your teeth, still white in the night.

I would like to tell you that it is funny how it all happened. It could not have happened any other way, except that it should have happened *every* other way—the odds were all against us. But we were the Universe's only choice. This—coming together— is how karma works.

> **"I am looking for friends. What does that mean— tame?"**
>
> **"It is an act too often neglected," said the fox.**

~

"It means to establish ties."

"To establish ties?"

"Just that," said the fox. "To me, you are still nothing more than a little boy who is just like a hundred thousand other little boys. And I have no need of you. And you, on your part, have no need of me. To you I am nothing more than a fox like a hundred thousand other foxes. But if you tame me, then we shall need each other. To me, you will be unique in all the world. To you, I shall be unique in all the world…"

~ Antoine de Saint-Exupéry, Le Petit Prince.

Chapters end. This chapter of my life has been a song of poverty, cell phone, solitude, laptop, americanos, bars, parties, dating, Dharma, dog, house, charm, community, workworkwork, bouldering, baths, movies, yoga, travel for work, success.

Time has faked left, run right—though it may not seem to move, it cannot wait for me.

I would like to continue to enjoy this chapter of lovers, but it must end: like the last notes of the bugle playing taps to wake an encampment of warriors to a Good Morning, or a Good Evening beneath fading, or rising stars.

I cannot wait for you. I am hungry and I need you. We each deserve the full: friendship, passion, love, family and service.

"*Now*" by its nature cannot wait, but it proceeds. Love may wait for one season, but not for two.

For a decade I have worked and worked. And when I finally look up I see my friends are older. Some of them move in together, some of them have babies, some of them have whitening hair, some of them build powerful businesses, some of them work as hard as I do, too…so we do not see each other for years…and before you know it we are hardly friends. My hair is still all bright, but soon enough, one Winter morning, my copper beard will have white in it.

You are young so you do not know, yet, though you can guess: life goes on and our once-young friends peer out from elderly faces with childlike eyes, wondering, *How did I get here? I am still who I have always been, but now I am an old person!* My friends live life, even as I work my days away: they have barbeques, they raise children or fall in love. They move to Olive City or Red Roof City or Independence City or Hipster City or Fog City or, now, Cow City—while I bike home.

In a few months I will visit you or you will visit me or neither: we will skip our stones into the river of life and the ripples will disappear and our two rocks will sink to the bottom and the river will flow on. The river may wend left or right but it does not wait.

I have set my king mattress on a few untreated pallets that a friend cut to fit. You should visit. I will offer you the guest room, which is red, and wood-paneled, and sunny yet cozy and we will make your bed and never need to remake it.

I would like to kiss into love. I am wearily desperate to relax into someone and just be. Our long-distance romance and our initial insecurities upon first meeting will both disappear like those two rocks skipped onto that river—when we touch. When we touch my body and your soft body, your dark tart cherry nipples, my freckled cheekbones. Your silly animal sounds, my tiger eyes. Your clothes will be lost in the sheets until tomorrow.

"I can be someone's and still be my own."
~ Shel Silverstein

I only met you the other day, but I have known you. I do not remember the particulars, but I do remember the little fire behind your eyes. I would like to curl up in front of our fire, and you would like to curl up within me. We are both tigers.

I remember you: I remember the give and take in the music of our conversation.

I would like to precisely remember your red smile.

I would like to remember the way you express a childlike freshness uncompromised by life's rough edges. You are, somehow, like this newly opened leaf, reborn each Spring, still wet, sticky, glimmering in anticipation at life.

I cannot wait to know you, but waiting will force our friendship to grow, and friendship is the core of our affection—not our

~

evident passion, not my eagerness to rest, not our connection borne of auspicious coincidence, not even our shared, rocky path of service.

"Hold the sadness and pain of samsara in your heart— and at the same time the power and vision of the Great Eastern Sun. Then, the warrior can make a proper cup of tea."
~ Pema Chödrön, paraphrasing Chögyam Trungpa.

Things I would like to do when I feel Alone.

"This is what you shall do; Love the earth and sun and the animals, despise riches, give alms to every one that asks, stand up for the stupid and crazy, devote your income and labor to others, hate tyrants, argue not concerning God, have patience and indulgence toward the people, take off your hat to nothing known or unknown or to any man or number of men, go freely with powerful uneducated persons and with the young and with the mothers of families, read these leaves in the open air every season of every year of your life, re-examine all you have been told at school or church or in any book, dismiss whatever insults your own soul, and your very flesh shall be a great poem and have the richest fluency not only in its words but in the silent lines of its lips and face and between the lashes of your eyes and in every motion and joint of your body." ~ Walt Whitman

~

I have burned out.

My mind has a *hummm* in it, like an overheated laptop or muted television. It is funny how quietly the burnout descended upon me. Twelve or sixteen or eighteen hours a day looking at electric-lit blue screens, seven days a week for eleven years…and I find my hands shake, my mind is fragmented, unable to settle and rest on the river bottom. I am always tired, now: though my energy still roars like the Canyon Waterfall, it is muffled, out of sight. Now, when I am charming as I am wont to be, in company, I feel fake.

All I want to do is nothing, for some time.

One more hire, a few more months, and I will get to be human, again. It will take many little tricks to stay on this horse, but I am good at this and have already barebacked many miles. I am aching and weary but it has been a good path.

Love without service is selfish.

Service without love is this path that I have traveled and while it is long and quiet and sometimes bitter, it is not one I regret.

> *"Not till we are lost, in other words not till we have lost the world, do we begin to find ourselves, and realize where we are and the infinite extent of our relations."*
> *~ Henry David Thoreau*

You are delighted in life, conscious of your sexuality; you are an artist. Poised: there are things in you that are sad and rich and sweet and fun.

Know that there are things you will not like about me.

While I love to dance, and am good at it—I do not get much practice so I may be clumsy. I struggle with my diet—eating too much or too little or not exercising enough when I work too much. I am a bear in the morning before coffee—keep me at arm's length, or laugh at me, for I tend to grump and growl. You will have to deal with the storm in my heart, if you want me. You will have to deal with my ambitions, and my humor.

I would like you to feel my tiredness, and not to shy away, but to take me in and see that I am weathered on the inside, too—beaten, rain streaming against a window.

I would like you to see that I have been a boulder on the side of the river—I have not changed my day-to-day life though others have changed so much.

I have a house. I have a dog sleeping three feet from me. Otherwise, my outward life has not changed in a decade. I am still building community, still going on dates with women who are still the same age, still doghiking the sage green red pink Mountain above my tall cozy home. I have not changed, and I am left behind; and yet I am current in ways those who have stepped out of the current are not current. My world expands outward, while their world grows within.

Loneliness is not merely romantic. It is a cold thing to get cozy in. This broken-open heart is our path. We are not afraid of traveling alone, you and I.

Loneliness is only a threat when we conflate it with lack of self-worth.

I would like for us to agree that focus—whether at work, in a relationship, as a parent…helps us to build beautiful things that matter. Some of us build things but we lay folks off, throw big parties, and promote profitable waste and disease in society. But some among us build human beings: we are parents, or teachers, or we run non-profits or nurture successful businesses that benefit society.

Whatever we build, our focus leads us to miss important things.

What is more important: to live life fully, or to change the world for the better?

Both, you quickly say.

But our own lives do not reflect "both."

For sometimes a choice must be made—this is the definition of *focus. Sacrifice* is not a word: it is loss and achievement, and most of all it is caring about *other* more than *self*. It takes Mad Ones with ascetic drive to cultivate something bigger than self-concern.

How many Saturdays do we get, in this lifetime?

On Saturday my trotting Red dog and a best friend and I go for a walk below the mountain, and along the creek that curls around and into town. It is raining lightly.

We talk about work and success, and dating and defeats—and laugh about it all. Friendships are like this: they take the bad things and dip them into a bowl of golden *ziji*. Alchemy:

> *"Ziji: a Buddhist term for brilliance, confidence, charisma, glamour, grace, overwhelming presence, resplendent radiance...A person possessed fully of the blessings and health that come from on high is said to be 'full of splendor.' This majesty is an authentic presence that envelops a healthy and prosperous warrior." ~ Shambhala*

The sky above us is bluegray, grayblue. The yellow, white, pinkwhite, red, purple wildflowers obstinately persevere in sunny optimism. It will snow, tomorrow—a heavy snow full of water.

But I, like these silly flowers, have persevered. For I have been trained all my life in the present moment. I have read stories of heroes, and I have read too many headlines that all agree: our wonderful world is under assault. Elephants, tigers, rhinos all extinct by the time this new generation has children. Disease-bearing plastic consumed by fish, birds and humans alike.

⁓

Acidifying oceans swelling with melting ice. Politics: a playing field for petty hate, not genuine dialogue. This is the best of times; this is the worst of times—this is a time for modest heroes.

If we have been given much, it is our duty to help others. In so doing, service waters our hearts with joy, no matter how cold we feel.

Selfish love is not the point of this life. Service with love is. Community is wealth.

> *"I slept and dreamt that life was joy. I awoke and saw that life was service. I acted and behold, service was joy."*
> *~ Rabindranath Tagore*

Walking below the mountain and along the creek, my friend and I walk into town. We sit down on the patio at my favorite farm-to-table restaurant for a late lunch. We are well-liked in this Small City, so sitting outside makes it impossible to be private—we are washed over by a shallow stream of stop n'chats.

I am too tired today to enjoy popularity: its saccharine joy comes with a bitter aftertaste.

The draws on my energy as I ride this path of service are endless. I have not taken the time to rest, enough—my discipline has been to find rest within the routine of my life, as it is.

Another friend joins us, and I feel how my popularity is thin.

Things I would like to do when I feel Alone.

〜

I have willingly sacrificed it—skipping parties, events, weddings so that I could focus. But I find that when I serve instead of play, I am no longer remembered by my community.

The gray rainy day makes me cold. I pull on an old white and blue striped wool sweater with a hole in the elbow.

〜

I am sad, today, so sad I fear I make others sad in my path, but my sadness is not badness, it is tiredness, for you are my water, and I have traveled long in this life without you.

Are you tired for me, too?

"Oh, darling, please stay by me. Please stay by me and see me through this." ~ Ernest Hemingway

Things I would like to do Before I Leave You.

"The woods are lovely, dark and deep,

But I have promises to keep,

And miles to go before I sleep,

And miles to go before I sleep."

~ Robert Frost

I would like to do it all with you before I leave you. I would like to live this life entire with you, before we leave one another.

I would spend my every morning with you, our friendship renewed each day with hot sunshine flooding through open windows, streaming through white linen curtains. Until we are white-haired and slow.

Your eyes will always be young. I will sit on my favorite

armchair and watch baseball on the television and holler at our grandchildren to get out of the way and go play outside!

Love is music, but it is literary, too.

Love is loneliness, an empty glass—but the glass may be empty because two lovers drank it, naked before the hot fireplace the night before.

I want you now.

I want you today.

I am willing to overlook your mistakes, if you overlook mine.

No: I will see all and you will see all and we will talk about it. Or make love about it. Or eat a lunch, silently, in white sunshine, avocado and sriracha on toast, with a side of greens I bought for you at the farmers' market this morning.

eat with me

It is Saturday. I could spend all day exploring your back.

The nape of your neck, my tongue exploring your white teeth and wet mouth, your eyes blinking butterflies at me, your hair all messed up just after you had taken the trouble to straighten it so carefully. I do not approve of your straightening it: I want you as close to being you as possible, because I like you.

I like you so I could read a chapter of Huck Finn to you, or Fitzgerald, or Kerouac. I like you so I would like to hear you read the books *you* love to me: your books are boringly unknown to me but because they come from your heart up through your throat out your mint-scented lips into this air, I find enthusiasm for them now, too. They are part of my world, now, too.

It is tomorrow, now, we lived today so fully we tired it out.

If you asked me what I would like to do, which you do not, for you are lost in your pleasant dreams of us—well, I would like to walk through wildflowers and set up a hammock and read one of my books in it and fall asleep, the sleep of one who has worked too hard for too long and lost too much and won more.

If you join me you will curl onto me and sleep beneath the leaves, too. It is the sleep of two lovers, face to face, close, silent, fully open like daisies turned calmly up into enough sun.

I would like to devour you so many times and you will consume me and we will visit one another so thoroughly we had better bring a backpack full of safety, or we will get started on future plans before we would like. Our hungers must flow up and

~

down, if they did not this teeter totter would only totter, and our match would go out. Your hunger is greater than mine, at times. Our appetites entwine, braiding up and down, when I am tired you are tigress, when I am tiger you have a small soft smile on one edge of your sleepy mouth.

I would like to go out with you, in my town where I know everyone—but I do not introduce you. I have introduced all the others and you are special and they will be able to tell.

I would like to visit you, alone, leaving my town behind. The middle of your woods, *your* cabin, your captain's chairs on your porch, your favorite forest walk.

My edges are rounded: like wood that has lived in water for too long, I am stronger now, I do not" succumb to self-pity and I do not float. How am I still strong? I am actually soft.

When the winds storm, I take down my sail. When the winds blow steadily, I raise it, again. I do not mind getting wet, I enjoy it and *whoop* and *yawp*. My expectations have been lowered by a long line of beautiful women who may be right for some handsome lover, but not for me. On empty nights I wonder if I am sailing over the horizon, alone.

My expectations totter because they are too high. Meaning: I want a match, no less, and I do not find it, so I no longer expect it. So you are like an extra pint of coconut ice cream, a welcome rain shower on a hot Summer's afternoon in this mountain valley, a flourish at the end of a calligraphed sentence! You are something extra that I did not and could not expect. You are a human being; you are my friend.

My past relationships are like how I enjoy piling cans one on top of another in the grocery line until they are almost as high as my head—too high, and they would all fall down.

Even if you were open, now, which you are not—we would probably not work. The odds are low. It is not likely.

But she who will match me will not be a game. She will be strong, from old stock, bare feet in the forest, red brick, worn brass, wide bark, polished cobble stone. She will be a craft, not a matter of odds.

Your legs beneath a short black dress, old-fashioned glasses, hair in a bun, laughter, open mouth and white teeth and chatter with a lovely friend and tea and cheap honey, your mug too hot to the touch for a few minutes.

I sit wearing a white and navy checkered cowboy shirt, in a worn out rocking chair, in short shorts, and flip flops, leaning back carefully into the old brick. This brick has stood here for a hundred years, with waxed-moustached drunks in dusty top hats riding by on silly bicycles or nodding horses. And now teenagers with Snapchat and Instagram stumble by, too self-enamored for the present moment.

I would like to take the back of your neck in my hand and cradle it.

231.

~

You would like my friends and I would like your friends and I would ignore your friends and you would ignore my friends and it is okay, either way. We are not clingy. When you flirt with my friends I will flirt with your friends, see if you like it. If you cross the line however I will leave a shadow behind, and never return. I am not one for games or jealousy, drama is unethical.

I would like to be alone with you and alone without you. Our social life would be like the seasons: fast Summer, engaged Autumn, cozy Winter, joyful Spring. I have unbuttoned your summerdress to see your breasts. Your bare feet are grounded, your character is settled, your words precise as birds' songs: precise like good jazz, not rigid or careful.

Let us start by your coming to me or my going to you. I am good at cutting through time-space—the only thing holding us back is our dating others, and your hesitation. I will fly to you and rent a room for a week and a bicycle and make trouble in your city. Or I will send a dragon to you and you will ride it to me for a date in the castle. My dragon friend will have you back within the hour after our first date. No need to blow dry your hair. Just hold on tight and wear spandex beneath your ball gown.

We cannot know if it will work but we can play—our destiny, a rippling banner taut in the wind.

If you want to visit, do so, or if you want me to visit I would like to do so, or if we want to adventure somewhere (hot springs, bicycle tour, learning to surf and snorkel), just say the word and I will make it.

"The beginning of love is to let those we love be perfectly themselves, and not to twist them to fit our own image. Otherwise we love only the reflection of ourselves we find in them." ~ Thomas Merton

You are not my dream girl.

You are this earth. You are not a fantasy: you are who I would like to dance with. And our love is this friendship lit by a wooden match with white on red. I am your match, and you are mine. And so we dance!

We will circle this globe together, going to the hard-to-get-to places, and if we come out the other side then our adventure will continue.

But it begins now.

Rrrrrrrinnnnng my doorbell. I will open my door. Like two hungry tigers, we patiently wait at the edge of the jungle. There are many animals to pounce upon but I do not want them. I would like to, together with you, make a meal and sit down to eat with a lit candle leaning into a golden candlestick.

Tigers do not eat tigers—they make love to them.

chapter twenty-seven.

Things I would like to do when I am Away.

"Absence is to love what wind is to fire; it extinguishes the small, it enkindles the great." ~ Roger de Rabutin

Our beginning has been literary. We write notes to one another but we have not kissed.

And now I am half a world away, yet your notes reach me just as quickly, and my notes reach you just as quickly. I would like to continue to remember you from time to time as I travel, and write you new notes as if in arching gray graphite pencil as if on a scrap of paper.

Here are these scraps of paper: they tell of my past relationships and chapters and bring you to Now, so that you will know all of me and so that I may let go of all of me and leap into an unknown future with you, hand in hand.

~

I am on the road. I am alone: surrounded by strangers, friendly strangers, and friends. But you are with me in your absence.

I would like to continue this lonely traveling; it is rich.

This morning: an old heavy green military bicycle, a light-weight blue sweater, a light-colored blue cotton oxford dress shirt. My body is fit and ready, it is Summer again, and I have learned to ask questions and make conversation with strangers.

In my home country we are different. Or perhaps it is this mode of traveling: here on the road it is not a bother to bother a stranger with small talk or a question of directions. Or perhaps it is that *I* am different, and they can tell I am a stranger. And strangers see me and become friendly.

Still, I see my home country everywhere: how they wear headphones to block out their world, how they drop plastic on their perfect talcum powderlike beach, how they listen to our worst songs and read about our celebrities.

When a song transports us back to past lovers and sweet days and sad hearts, I think of *her* with appreciation, then snap back to here, wherever I am—and I feel gratitude for *you*, now.

Do you feel a small part of yourself traveling with me?

I am in a gray city full of strong stone buildings with gloriously unnecessary architecture, and necessary craftsmanship that is as good today as when it was built and shaped centuries ago.

I would like to take these moments to write you this note, and pin it up for you—then I must get out and run around, and fill my eyes with newness.

I am writing you from a spacious well-loved white and cement café, formerly a warehouse.

You should do nothing

that you do not wish to do

you should,

however,

be here with me.

Nick Drake is singing softly, sadly, before his end.

The quiet roar of the silver espresso machine,

strange Northern pastries with cardamom,

gray morning light.

A dog in the café, waiting to play outside

bicycles, tattoos, thick sweaters.

A white candle dripping neatly on my gold table.

All of it so new and yet so cool, so familiar,
this world of ours.

The uncertainty in our literary love is enough, for now. But not for long—for I am no coward, I am a gentle man—and

~

you are no dilettante, you are a wolf.

I would like to tell you about my journey from far away, for it is romantic to be alone without you, and yet to feel so close to you…

The girls play guitar and fiddle and sing softly in high lilting laughing voices across the street and I stomp with disarming charming abandon!

The girls sway in their shirt dresses with thin belts and olive skin and perfectly dark green eyes that hold my gaze, and smile around it. They remind me that we need not be shy in our affection. They are strong in their openness—not weak. They are fiercely hungry for all that is good to eat.

Let's unlearn.

There is nothing wrong with corny. Mushy. Cheesy. We learned to be tough in school. It is good to be tough. But! It is good to have a tough spine behind an open heart. It is good to remember that there is no vulnerability in complete openness. If we are all the way open there is nothing to hit.

Openness is tough.

Machismo is ginned-up fear.

Relaxing is tough.

~

Our future life does not exist, except in the seeds we planted yesterday when I invited you to join me for my birthday month.

Tomorrow, and the tomorrow after that, and ten tomorrows after that, and a thousand tomorrows and moon cycles from now, if we cultivate this garden we may grow a life co-mingled. We are not likely, but love is not a thing of odds—it is a thing to make happen if we wish to make it so.

This is how all great affairs have arisen.

"I had three chairs in my house; one for solitude, two for friendship, three for society."
~ Henry David Thoreau, Walden.

I would like to pay a caring sweet slow old craftsman to build up a tiny house, up in the big tree in my backyard out of good old things. I would like for it to be made entirely out of local things with history and therefore quality in them. It will be raised high above the ground so the rain and the earth can still meet. This tiny tree house will sit on a tiny deck that will be set upon another, larger deck ten feet below.

If you are mad at me or when I am mad at you or if you want to write or I want to write or you want to do yoga on the balcony or I want to read in the tree or if I want to sleep separately (maybe I am sick and when I am sick I may snore), well, you or I can go up into the treehouse.

And I can host an occasional guest in the warmer months and use it however I would like.

Space is a good gift to give one another.

Red dog can dig holes down under and lie in the cool shade. And on the roof I will plant xeriscapeable plants except for one section, which will hold a skylight so we can stare back up at the stars as we fall asleep. The walls will be full of little shelves and inset century-old stained glass windows.

The view of the mountains cradling the sky from above my tiny tree home will be mind-pausing.

Things I would like to do with You in the End just Before the Beginning.

"There are times to cultivate and create, when you nurture your world and give birth to new ideas and ventures.

There are times of flourishing and abundance, when life feels in full bloom, energized and expanding.

And there are times of fruition, when things come to an end. They have reached their climax and must be harvested before they begin to fade.

And finally of course, there are times that are cold, and cutting and empty, times when the spring of new beginnings seems like a distant dream.

Those rhythms in life are natural events. They weave into one another as day follows night, bringing, not messages of hope and fear, but messages of how things are."
~ *Chögyam Trungpa*

I daydream of then, when I was with you.

When, in the evening the woodpecker knocks and asks me my age, I say "Halfway to death; Halfway to birth." And it nods its head again and again.

I would like to return to our fine romance.

I would like to return to the past.

I would like to return to our dream cabin in the woods up in the foothills, where I first rested into your heart.

But I cannot continue to daydream, for I have living to do and the stream, it pauses for no one.

So I would like to take our dream fort down, and I would like to take the dead flowers from the dry Ball jars and crush them and drop them into the young rose bush outside.

I would like to make another orange fire when it is dark—after I hammock and read until it is too dark to read and the mosquitoes will not let me read any longer. I would like to drink rich scotch given to me awhile ago by a good friend. Red dog curls up close to the fire, and snores. He naps sixteen hours a day!

And so I would like to return to reality: to this present moment. I would like to return to my tall house on the long hill above my Small City. I would like to stay in this sad present instead of living in our pleasant dreams. I would like to float forward, along with this life's waves: for genuine sadness may be bitter mint, but put it in too-cold water and it becomes cheerful, too.

And so I put away those things that remind me of loving you. I would like to wrap and tie our love into a bundle, and set it gently into the farmers' stream above my house so that our memories may float until they sink, free again as they were when we breathed life into our future: sweating, smiling, sighing.

~

I had never been much good at crying. I went years without crying. Now I can *almost* cry, which almost feels good. When I meet you I will cry and cry: it will feel so good. But for now, I still feel this sadness behind my eyes, a reservoir pressing up against a dam. I am waiting for you.

When I remember them I am sad; I am not angry. I happily loved her and her, a little, and she and she loved me, a little, and we made love, a little, and we laughed, and we argued only a few times and made up quickly: except for the last time.

The last time always broke each of us—and they joined the line walking slowly away from me.

She had said it was all too much too fast, one too many times— and that was when I hopped off our rollercoaster.

~

I am ready for one who enjoys the ride, and breathes—laughs!—through her fear at the giddiness of it.

Her naked self below me her arrival in the park her blue dress and khaki corduroy hat with orange letters: it was a meeting to mint a memory and she is forgotten and what was between us fades.

At the end, after our lives have joined our love and dissipated into the sky above, all that is left are knick-knacks: precious things of no value, curiosities of momentous momentary moments to be put into cardboard boxes by someone who knows nothing of their meanings. The boxes daisychained into someone's SUV and donated away.

We will be gone: if it all dies away, does love matter?

Hai!

For that is for the future of the Past: what I have learned from her, and her, and her will shape my ability to love you, fully.

~

All that matters now is to live while the moment lasts, and then to hop onto the next moment.

> *"To ease the pain of living. Everything else, drunken dumbshow." ~ Allen Ginsberg*

I would like to see your face but you are silhouetted against the sun, the blindingly bright ocean of the Future at your back. I appreciate the shape of your dress.

I would like to see your expression: your open eyes, your proud nose, I would like to tuck your hair behind your ear, I would like to hear your blue voice, I would like to touch your long hand.

And I would like to be alone, for now, for the Winter is about to come, and it is not yet time for our Future.

I would like to know if I already know your name. I already know your last name: what is mine is yours, though you do not have to have it.

I would like to hear your laugh, it is awkward but not self-conscious. I would even like to hear you smile in your sleep, a quiet smile.

Red dog will be in the corner, he will be older now, and he will snore more, and when he does we think it is sweet and funny.

I would like to stretch you out below and be stretched out above, and we can turn and toss, and bend and jump, and

⁓

ride and stand, and bend and laugh, and pray.

I would like to look into your eyes without thinking any thing.

"Whosoever is delighted in solitude is either a wild beast, or a god." ~ Sir Francis Bacon, via Aristotle.

Ah, finally.

I would like to celebrate this life with someone—but I would like to keep my Alone, too…Alone is the earth beneath the roots beneath the flower beneath the rain and sunshine.

I would like to love, but I have lost many dear friends and shallow friends and I would like to take the time to fully appreciate my own being and I think that this is enough. But it may not be, but it had better be or I shall turn bitter, and that would be understandable. For human society is a cold thing. I am tired of serving those who would burn their own nest.

Here, Winter is coming in now—I can see it rising over the mountains, falling down at our Big Town. And I will close in, with Red dog. I will close the doors, and I will shut the windows, and I will turn off the water and bring all the wood in. I would like to use my kindling axe.

I would like to plan a party in my home: friends and families will come and stand in white cotton or gray wool or funny-colored socks on my red rugs and sit on my old-fashioned wingback armchairs. And three children will sit tightly together in my little rickety antique settee, holding some dear friend's newest baby. And five of us will venture out to the park above and the now-dry farmers' stream and gather snow and bring it back and we would like to pour maple syrup on the snow and serve it up. And someone will make hot tea, and we will sing or toast and talk loudly, and later a few of us will tromp along wet snowy roads with Red dog talking about forgettable things.

> *"Sexiness wears thin after a while and beauty fades, but to be married to a man who makes you laugh every day, ah, now that's a real treat."*
> *~ Joanne Woodward, on living with Paul Newman.*

It is now white Winter.

It is nearly the Future. Though I do not like sunglasses I will wear them as I snowshoe up to my cold cabin, through naked stark dark trees.

My strong legs are shaky with hunger—I am defeated today, yet still I can win.

My hunger makes me focused, dangerous. It is cold, so I wear the union suit beneath the striped sweater and the hat and the jeans and the too-heavy boots with soft linings and the tweed jacket and the coat with its high collar over the bottoms of my pink ears. A cozy Winter is about breathable layers.

⁓

When Winter leaves and the fog comes and the rain comes and when the leaves come, budding neon green…then perhaps we will meet our match, and be alone, together, and become dear to one another: fearless servants devoted to the commonwealth.

I would like that.

My weariness may not calcify into self-pity: instead it must give me resolve. This metal has been polished by years of loneliness. The heat, your smile, our caring…will light the fire in our cabin in the woods and our story will ripple for generations.

You had better watch yourself: time is coming for us.

> *"And History, with all her volumes vast,*
> *Hath but one page, — 'tis better written here…*
> *All treasures, all delights, that eye or ear,*
> *Heart, soul could seek, tongue ask —*
> *Away with words! draw near…"*
> *~ Lord Byron*

A List of
Things I would like to do with You.

I would like to miss you,

I would like to do things without you.

I would like to work together but apart with you—at a café in the cool shade with Red dog napping on the cool redrock, below our feet.

I would like to finish and then have sex with you again, after a moon-watching pause.

I would like to bring you breakfast in bed, with the Sunday paper, only once in a long while.

I would like for you to make me black coffee, often.

I would like to road trip to hot springs with you and camp the night in a canvas tent and listen to the winded trees with you.

~

I would like to bicycle tour with you.

I would like to dinner with our friends and our families along an endless table on an endless lawn, with you.

I would like for you to please never hide your simple beauty.

I would like to cradle our first child with you, and talk over how to discipline her in a way that inspires her when she is older.

I would like to argue over our fourth child's name, and for you to let me think I won, again.

I would like to be surprised at how often you laugh with me.

I would like to cook with you just about every day.

I would like be uncomfortable in a hammock with you, trying to read.

I would like you to keep your hair wild even when you grow old.

I would like to feel admiration for the littlest things you do: say, how you look others in the eyes, openly, with warmth.

I would like you to be careful when doing dangerous things.

I would like for you to care for the truth above comfort.

I would like for you to be patient and forgiving of others—and when you are impatient, to be forgiving of yourself.

I would especially like be bored with you.

I would like to be angry with you, and huff and puff and have you fail to take me seriously.

I would like to go to sleep each night by thanking you for being with me, even if I do not mean it, and wake each morning pleasantly surprised to find you in my life.

Forever is not important to me, but this is.

The End.

About the Author.

Photo: Tanya Dueri

Waylon Lewis likes to think he snowshoes hut-to-hut and builds nail-less tiny houses in trees while drinking wild-crafted teas from herbs he has gathered in the woods beside his faithful half-hound, Redford. In reality he works on a laptop, rarely travels, drinks black coffee, eats vegan without preaching about it (much), bikes 365 days a year, climbs lazily, yogas clumsily and runs *Elephant Journal*. He knows little about love.

Born in Boulder to a poor and generous single mom, he trained in Buddhism, lived in Vermont, studied stuff in Boston, worked at Shambhala this & that, then founded elephant. His only real ambition is to help create enlightened society through words.

Acknowledgments.

Writing is hard. Except for when it's not—sometimes it comes easy. Either way, if our writing comes from a genuine place it's always fun, or fulfilling. In my experience, if we're on the right track, writing is cathartic. A fundamental kind of joy.

But writing a book is hard, full stop.

Especially when, as in the case of the book you now hold in your hands, one chooses to forgo publishers (even those sweet kind ones who show interest) and design the book and book cover and print in the USA on ecopaper and buy offsets in the form of one tree planted for every single book purchased.

Reinventing the wheel is hard. Swimming upstream against a cynical publishing world is hard. Doing something mindfully is often hard.

Folks don't get as excited as they would if I had gone with a conventional publisher ("you've been published, wow!" sounds cooler than "you're publishing yourself, hunh?") and distribution is hard without Amazon and big box stores and the backing of a corporate publisher and a PR team paid to say how great you are. But ultimately most of that is hype and noise, sound and fury. Doing things slowly, in our speedy world, can be more fulfilling.

~

And this book happened, nevertheless. And the next books will be easier—this one was the first guinea pig in what is now *Elephant Books* (find us on Facebook).

This book happened because the writing connected with readers. I'd never experienced such a reaction as when I published what would become the first chapter of this book. It happened because 108,000 of you liked our Facebook page (find *Things I would like to do with You* on Facebook) before this was even a book. It happened because this book tapped into something we all care about: *love.* A love that includes room for change, humor, even a little loneliness. Our generation is looking for a love that isn't claustrophobic, that isn't fantasy-based, that isn't founded on brittle *Mad Men* gender roles. We all want a love that is real and raw.

On an earthy level, however, this book happened because of Lindsey Block. She edited every word of this book four or five times, at least. Without her steadfast belief in it and in me as a writer and a boss and a friend, this book would still just be a bunch of surprisingly-popular blogs on elephantjournal.com, where we have worked together now for seven years.

This book happened because of Emily Bartran, who loves words as much as I do and helped me choose "littlest" vs. "little" and a thousand other little editorial decisions that helped this book to rise above, or rather fall beneath cliché. Clichés and love are a dangerously easy combination.

~

This book happened because of other colleagues who also edited and consulted and pushed me: Bryonie Wise, Sara Crolick, Rachel Nussbaum and Meredith Meeks (who filmed and edited our *Things* video), and Pam Uhlenkamp (who I've worked with for, sheesh, thirteen years. She designed the book you just read).

This book happened because of those women who have loved me, and lost me (or, more likely, I lost them). I have learned from them, and laughed with them, and I have loved and been loved by them…and this book is what I have learned.

But most of all this book happened because of the vision and kindness of Chögyam Trungpa, my sweet mom's Buddhist teacher, who offered a vision of love as a journey—a partnership—a vision of love as something tender, and playful, and unselfish.

"Love does not consist in gazing at each other, but in looking outward together in the same direction."
~ Antoine de Saint-Exupéry

About the Bookiness of this Book.

We all love books. We all love independent bookstores. But the physical creation of a book, these days, is horrible.

Most (nearly all) books are printed overseas, plastic-coated, with toxic glues and toxic inks. Vegetable inks are better, but still kind of toxic. Paper is chlorine-ful (which kills biodiversity in our watersheds). Books are carbon-heavy to ship, and bookstores return most (unsold) books. Finally, recycling plastic and toxic books is energy-intensive and toxic.

But there's good news! *Elephant Books* seeks to undo all that bad stuff. The book you hold in your hands is about the quiet power of Nature and true love. I therefore could not print with a Big Publisher (they print plastic, toxic, overseas). So we went our own way. Our hard-won achievements include: printing in the USA (and, locally!—22 blocks from my home); keeping the cover plastic-free; using 30% recycled, 100% chlorine-free, 100% sustainably-managed carbon-sucking paper with veggie-based inks; and offsetting *every* book and its shipping with a donation to save an orphaned elephant baby (Sheldrick Trust).

Finally, Amazon is a book bully: bad for publishers, authors and readers (google *"New Yorker: 'Cheap Words'"*). I am therefore distributing this book independently. If you are inspired, use #thingsiwouldliketodowithyou on twitter, Facebook or Instagram or invite a friend to get a copy: elephantjournal.com/books.

Benefactors.

Things is Amazon-free (*why? Read "Cheap Words" on thenewyorker.com*) & corporate publisher-free (*no mainstream book published in the US is eco, but we wanted to be*). Without The Man's muscle, *Things* depended on its serialization on *Elephant Journal*, its funding via Kickstarter, its community on Facebook (*where we had 108,000+ fans a year before publication*), orders by indie book stores (*want to offer Things in yours? Email: books@elephantjournal.com*) & the enthusiasm (& patience) of…you. Finally, five readers lifted this book up:

Monika Carless

Jud Valeski

Debi Jordan

Harish Nim

Brad Feld